Women of Achievement

Venus and Serena Williams

Women *of* Achievement

Abigail Adams

Susan B. Anthony

Tyra Banks

Clara Barton

Hillary Rodham Clinton

Marie Curie

Ellen DeGeneres

Diana, Princess of Wales

Helen Keller

Sandra Day O'Connor

Georgia O'Keeffe

Nancy Pelosi

Rachael Ray

Eleanor Roosevelt

Martha Stewart

Venus and Serena Williams

Women of Achievement

Venus and Serena Williams

ATHLETES

Anne M. Todd

CHELSEA HOUSE
PUBLISHERS
An imprint of Infobase Publishing

VENUS AND SERENA WILLIAMS

Chelsea House
An imprint of Infobase Publishing
132 West 31st Street
New York NY 10001

Library of Congress Cataloging-in-Publication Data
Todd, Anne M.
  Venus and Serena Williams : athletes / by Anne M. Todd.
    p. cm. — (Women of achievement)
  Includes bibliographical references and index.
  ISBN 978-1-60413-461-2 (hardcover)
  1. Williams, Venus, 1980—Juvenile literature. 2. Williams, Serena, 1981—Juvenile literature. 3. Tennis players—United States—Biography—Juvenile literature. 4. African American women tennis players—Biography—Juvenile literature. I. Title. II. Series.

  GV994.A1T64 2009
  796.3420922—dc22
  [B]

                                    2009000322

Chelsea House books are available at special discounts when purchased in bulk quantities for businesses, associations, institutions, or sales promotions. Please call our Special Sales Department in New York at (212) 967-8800 or (800) 322-8755.

You can find Chelsea House on the World Wide Web at http://www.chelseahouse.com

Series design by Erik Lindstrom
Cover design by Ben Peterson and Alicia Post

Printed in the United States of America

Bang EJB 10 9 8 7 6 5 4 3 2 1

This book is printed on acid-free paper.

All links and Web addresses were checked and verified to be correct at the time of publication. Because of the dynamic nature of the Web, some addresses and links may have changed since publication and may no longer be valid.

CONTENTS

1   Williams vs. Williams   7

2   Growing Up on the Courts   10

3   Going Professional   25

4   Rising in the Ranks   41

5   Making Dreams Come True   61

6   Keeping the Balance   72

7   A New Outlook   88

8   Looking Forward   102

Chronology   105

Notes   108

Bibliography   115

Further Resources   122

Index   124

About the Author   128

Picture Credits   128

Williams
vs. Williams

The year was 2008. The event was the U.S. Open, one of the most important tennis tournaments of the year. On this late-summer day, the crowd at Arthur Ashe Stadium in New York City was abuzz. They were about to watch what might have been the most entertaining match between tennis superstars—and sisters—to date: the quarterfinal match between Venus Williams and Serena Williams.

When the sisters walked onto the court with their tennis rackets in hand, all eyes were on them. Venus, 28 years old and standing 6-foot-1, dressed in all black, has long arms and legs, a lean body, and a look of fierce determination. At the time, Venus was ranked seventh in the world. Serena, Venus's younger sister by 15 months, dressed in all red, is slightly shorter—standing 5-foot-11—and has a more

Serena Williams, right, shakes hands with her sister Venus Williams, after Serena wins their quarterfinal match at the U.S. Open tennis tournament in New York on September 3, 2008.

muscular figure, but she shares the same determination in her eyes. She was ranked fourth in the world.

The stakes were high. If Serena won, she would have a chance to regain her No. 1 ranking as the top women's tennis player in the world. If Venus won, she would have a chance to win another Grand Slam title.

Over their long tennis careers, the two sisters had met 16 times, with each winning eight matches. Despite this even record, past matches between the sisters were often lackluster. Their feelings for each other would sometimes prevent them from playing their best tennis.

That was not the case on this evening, as the match featured spectacular points and dramatic shifts in momentum. Venus took leads in both sets, holding two set points in the first and a remarkable eight set points in the second. (A set point occurs when the player who is leading needs one more point to win the set.) Serena chased down shot after shot to hold off Venus and come back in both sets. She ended up winning in two tiebreakers, 7-6, 7-6. Only two months before the U.S. Open, the sisters had faced each other at another important tournament—Wimbledon; in that face-off, Venus had won. But today was Serena's victory: She would move on, and Venus's U.S. Open was finished. Venus would later tell an interviewer, "I'm a very good closer. I've never had a match like that in my life. I guess there's always a first. [Serena] just played a little better."[1] Serena had been surprised by Venus's errors, many of which came on those set points, so Serena considered herself lucky. Although happy for her own success, Serena could feel for her sister. She said, "I try not to look at [Venus] because I might start feeling bad. I want the best for her. I love her so much. She's my best friend."[2]

Growing Up on the Courts

Venus Ebony Starr Williams was born on June 17, 1980, in Lynwood, California. A little more than a year later, on September 26, 1981, Serena Jameka Williams was born in Saginaw, Michigan. The girls are the daughters of Richard and Oracene Williams. They have three older half sisters who are Oracene's daughters. Richard and Oracene married in 1980. After Serena was born in 1981, while she was still an infant, the family of seven moved from Saginaw, Michigan, back to sunny Southern California.

Richard, a Louisiana native and the head of a private security firm, and Oracene, a nurse from Mississippi, raised their five girls—Lyndrea, Isha, Yetunde, Venus, and Serena—to believe in themselves. It was important for the Williams children to believe that they could make something of their lives, as the family lived in a rough, poverty-stricken city called Compton, located near Los Angeles. Compton was a high-crime area, known for drug sales and gangs, and the family witnessed much violence. Compton, though, was not all bad. Much of the city was filled with hardworking people trying to provide and care for their families on small incomes. Times were hard, and money was tight. Richard believed that living in such conditions would prepare his children for the harsh realities of the world and make them better able to handle all kinds of situations.

RICHARD WILLIAMS

Richard knew what it was like to live in poverty. In Shreveport, Louisiana, where he grew up with his mother (his father was rarely around) and his sisters—Patty, Barbara, Penny, and Fay—his family had little. His mother worked as a cotton picker in the summer months and as a custodian at a school during the rest of the year. When Richard was just 12 years old, he paid $75 for a small plot of land on which he built a simple house for his family. At the end of that year, he paid the balance of what he owed for the land—another $75. The house, like many in the area, had no running water or electricity.

Growing up in the segregated South during the 1940s and 1950s, Richard was accustomed to racism. White people often called him racist names. He was not allowed to ride in the front of buses. He was not allowed to eat in certain restaurants. He was not allowed to sit with white people in theaters. Despite the unfair treatment, Richard's mother taught him to rise above his surroundings and believe in himself. She taught him not to think of himself as a Negro (the term then used for African Americans) but to think of himself as a man—a man who could do and achieve whatever he set his mind to do. When he was 17, she encouraged him to get out of Louisiana. She was worried that he would be killed if he stayed. With a dollar in his pocket, Richard got on a freight train and left home.

He moved around a lot and took odd jobs where he could. He eventually met Oracene, and they fell in love and married. Richard tells people that, even before Venus or Serena were born, he had plans for them to become tennis stars. In the late 1970s, he was watching a women's tennis tournament on television and was amazed at the prize money the winner received—more than he made in an entire year. Richard decided then that he and Oracene should make their children into tennis stars.

Richard believed in taking charge of one's own life. He believed in going after what you wanted and making it happen. So, when he decided he wanted to know how to play tennis, he taught himself. He read books, watched videos, and studied matches on television. He got a ball machine and practiced his backhand and his forehand until he felt confident in his ability. He found an instructor—oddly enough, also named Richard Williams—who taught him how to move quickly and lightly on his feet and how to improve his strokes to give them more power and precision. Richard fell in love with the game. He wanted to share his love of tennis with those who mattered the most to him: his family.

First, Richard taught Oracene the game of tennis. Then, as soon as their daughters were old enough, Richard and Oracene took them to the public tennis courts in Compton. All of the girls learned the game. To the three older girls, tennis was not that much fun. Venus and Serena, however, had a love of the game and—as Richard soon discovered—a mountain of talent.

LEARNING THE GAME

Under their father's direction, Venus started to play tennis at age four; Serena learned to play a year later, when she, too, was four. Venus would later tell an interviewer that she does not remember learning how to play—she just remembers always knowing how to play. She was so young when she stepped onto the court that tennis has always felt a part of her life.

Once they were school age, the girls played tennis nearly every day. On weekdays, they would go directly to the courts from school. Richard and Oracene did not insist on this; the girls *wanted* to be on the court. They would hit balls over and over again, taking a break only to go home for dinner. Then they would return to the courts. Eventually, it would get dark and the girls would reluctantly head home, eager to begin the cycle the next day.

When Richard realized that his daughters' natural talent and drive could make them champions, he told them that they would someday win at Wimbledon, a prestigious tennis tournament in England. Venus and Serena believed him. And they wanted it. They both wanted to be the top-ranked player in the world. They worked hard to turn that dream into a reality, and Richard did all he could to prepare them.

IN HER OWN WORDS

The Williams sisters encourage people to pursue their dreams. As Serena said in the book *Venus & Serena: Serving from the Hip: 10 Rules for Living, Loving, and Winning*:

> Venus and I really like it when people tell us that they have big dreams. One of the most important things you can do for yourself is envision a fantastic future. Dreams give you direction in life. Everyone who is successful started with one.

Richard Williams practices with his daughter Serena in Compton, California, in 1991. Richard's motivation would inspire both Serena and Venus to reach their full potential as tennis players.

One way in which Richard tried to prepare his daughters was to insist that they play on the Compton courts. The courts were not in good shape—the pavement was cracked and the equipment was falling apart. The courts, too, were not known for their safety. Local gangs considered the courts part of their turf. When the Williams family first started to use the courts, Richard was frequently beaten up. But that did not stop him from returning. He was not going to show his daughters that it was all right to back down from their dreams. Richard held his ground and continued to show up until the gang members finally left him alone. The Williamses' presence on the courts became a regular sight. People came to expect to see them there.

Still, Richard kept his daughters prepared. At any sound that resembled a gunshot, the girls were taught to hit the ground. So even if a car backfired, the girls dropped to the ground. One time, a car drove by and a man fired a gun out of the sunroof. When Oracene heard about the shooting, practices at the Compton courts ended. Eventually, though, the girls returned. Gang activity was simply a part of life in Compton. Reportedly, Richard also paid children in the area to yell racial taunts at Venus and Serena to prepare them for the kind of prejudice they might face in the mostly white tennis world.

Richard was certain that Venus and Serena were going to be tennis stars. He knew they would often be in front of cameras. So Richard also prepared his daughters for the media by taking videos of them. While taping them, Richard would ask his daughters questions. Sometimes he would simply tape family picnics or the girls playing at home. The sisters became so used to the camera that they were not uncomfortable or self-conscious when their father would ask them specific questions about their tennis strokes or other aspects of the game.

Richard also looked to outside sources to help the girls achieve their potential in tennis. He devoted much of his own time and attention on Venus, because she was older and would be the first one ready for competition. Venus, like her father, also learned a lot about tennis from watching matches on television. From her observations, she learned that the best players figured out their opponents' weaknesses and then repeatedly hit the ball to that side. Venus also learned to incorporate other players' techniques in her game.

When Richard realized that he did not have enough time to devote to both girls equally, he asked James Pyler, a teacher at Inglewood High School who also played tennis, to help. Pyler was happy to offer his time. He worked with Serena, changing her forehand grip and helping her with her volleys. These changes improved Serena's game.

LIFE OUTSIDE OF TENNIS

Richard and Oracene instilled traditional values in their children. In fact, the couple acted much as their parents had; they placed great importance on hard work, dedication, good study habits, and self-discipline. Both parents

THE GAME OF TENNIS

Tennis is a sport that demands great endurance, speed, and power. Venus and Serena Williams have the strength and skill to be among the elite tennis players in the world. Playing tennis regularly can help keep people fit and healthy. The sport can also benefit a person's self-esteem and confidence. People young and old can learn to play tennis.

Tennis is played on a court with a net stretched across the middle. It can be played as singles, in which one player stands on each side of the net, or as doubles, in which two players stand on each side of the net. Players use a racket to hit the ball back and forth over the net. The ball can bounce only once before it must be returned. The object of the game is to win points against your opponent. A point continues until one player hits the ball into the net or outside the boundary lines.

A game's score is calculated as follows: 15, 30, 40, and game. (So 15 is 1 point, 30 is 2 points, 40 is 3 points, and game is 4 points. If a player has 0 points, it is called love.) If treated their children with love and respect; more than anything, they wanted a strong family unit in which everyone worked together and helped one another. Oracene taught her girls to find recognition from within themselves—not from other people. She devoted nearly all of her time to her girls' needs. Richard dedicated himself to teaching Venus and Serena the game of tennis, as well as lessons about surviving in an often racist world, standing up for your beliefs, planning your successes, and reaching for the top.

both players get to 3 points, the score is 40-40, or deuce. To win the game from deuce, one player must score the next 2 points in a row. If they win 1 point, but lose the next, the score goes back to deuce.

To begin a game of tennis, a player serves the ball from behind the baseline diagonally across to the opponent's service court. If the serve stays inbounds and the opponent fails to touch the ball, it is called an ace and the server wins the point. If the serve hits the net or goes out of bounds, it is called a fault. The server has a second chance to serve. If the server hits another fault, it is a double fault and the opponent scores a point.

To win a set, a player must win six games by a margin of two games. If the set reaches 6-6, a tiebreaker is played in most tournaments. Professional women's tennis matches are best-of-three sets. In the major tournaments, the men play best-of-five sets.

The Williamses are devout Jehovah's Witnesses. As members of this Christian group, which originated in the United States in the late 1800s, the Williamses do not participate in government affairs of any kind, would not serve in the military or accept a blood transfusion, and do not celebrate certain holidays or events, like Christmas or birthdays. The Williamses believe in putting God first, then family, and then education. (Tennis comes fourth.) When the girls were growing up, the family attended services about twice a week at Kingdom Hall. Venus has told interviewers that her strong association with her religion has resulted in her feeling grounded and connected with herself, her family, and her faith.

As a child, Serena idolized her older sister, Venus. All five sisters were very close and spent nearly all their time together. The five sisters shared a single room with four beds. As the youngest, Serena was the one who alternated which bed she slept in at night. Venus's was Serena's favorite. Serena wanted to do what Venus did, wear what Venus wore, and act as Venus acted. In fact, Serena looked up to Venus so much that when the family went out to a restaurant, their parents insisted that Serena order first so that she would be forced to choose something on her own instead of selecting what Venus ordered.

Because the Williams sisters were busy with schoolwork and tennis, they did not have time for Saturday morning cartoons or extended play dates at friends' houses. But each remembers her childhood fondly. They feel that their parents worked to make their lives well rounded—it wasn't all about tennis. Oracene strove to fill the house with fun, laughter, and smiles. The five sisters spent lots of time playing together in their backyard. They looked forward to the arrival of the ice cream truck, eagerly spending their allowance on treats. The neighborhood doughnut truck was popular, as well. The sisters also had fun trying out new physical activities, like roller-skating, tae kwon do, ballet, and gymnastics. Richard and Oracene knew that a tennis career was short-lived; it was not uncommon for a tennis player to play professionally for only a decade. The Williamses realized that Venus and Serena needed to develop interests outside of tennis to prepare for life after their playing careers ended.

Venus excelled in track as well as tennis. By 1989, she showed signs of being a great track star. She went undefeated in 19 meets as a sprinter and as a middle-distance runner. The year before she ran a mile in 5 minutes, 29 seconds. She also loved stickers and collected them in albums and boxes. Serena was interested in everything from skateboarding to sewing to playing guitar. Both Venus and Serena enjoyed fashion and design. In their teenage years, they would discover the fun of surfing. They enjoyed life and what it had to offer, but they always came back to tennis. Their deep love for the sport led them to put in long hours of practice. They enjoyed improving their game and watching each other develop into stronger, more confident players.

BEYOND COMPTON

Venus and Serena entered their first tennis tournaments when each was four-and-a-half. They played in weekend tournaments for the next five years, from 1985 to 1990. Serena won 46 of the 49 tournaments she entered, becoming the top-ranked player in the 10-and-under age group on Southern California's junior circuit. Venus won all 63 junior tournaments she entered. On the junior circuit, Venus often walked away with 6-0, 6-0 wins; she was ready for more advanced players. Venus became the top-ranked player in the 12-and-under class on the Southern California junior circuit when she was just 10 years old. Just a year later, she became the top-ranked player in the 14-and-under class.

In this August 1990 photo, Venus talks with her father, Richard Williams, during a practice session.

By July 1990, when Venus was 10, coaches, trainers, and agents from around the state thought she could become a teenage tennis superstar. They were impressed with the way she used her topspin forehand with precision and effectiveness. She hit hard, jumped high, and covered the court quickly and fluidly. She had more skill than many players far older than her. Tennis insiders wanted to see Venus enter more tournaments in preparation for turning professional. Venus's father, however, did not think that pushing his daughters to play more tournaments was a wise idea. He worried about Venus and Serena burning out. He also wanted them to be children—to live the lives of regular kids participating in many activities. So rather than increasing the number of tournaments they entered each year, he limited their tournament play. In the years that followed, people would question and criticize Richard's decision.

For the next few years, agents kept the pressure on the Williams family. They offered cars, houses, money—whatever they thought it would take to sign Venus Williams to a contract. Richard was not impressed. He told an interviewer, "I've talked to everybody, but I've signed with nobody. If we sign [Venus] to a professional contract when she's 10, what will she do between now and when she's 13, when she can actually play the professional circuit? I don't want her to peak at 12 and fall to pieces at 15. There's still a lot of ifs here. I've been broke all my life, and Venus doesn't want to be poor, but nobody in this house is going to push our daughter into anything."[1]

In September 1991, the Williams family moved to Florida. It was here that Rick Macci, a world-famous tennis instructor, coached elite players, including Mary Pierce and Jennifer Capriati. Before the move, Richard had asked Macci to come to Compton to see his daughters play. Macci watched the sisters and was especially struck by Venus's overall athleticism. When she asked to use the restroom, Venus walked partway there on her hands and then did a backflip to return to her feet. Macci could see that she possessed a natural ability similar to that of basketball great Michael Jordan. Macci offered Richard scholarships for Venus and Serena to live and train at his facility at Grenelefe Resort in Florida.

Richard agreed; he enrolled Venus and Serena in the Rick Macci International Tennis Academy. Here, Richard felt the girls would receive better instruction. He wanted them to focus on becoming good professional players rather than just playing tournaments.

When the family arrived in Florida in 1991, Macci provided the Williamses with a home and tennis lessons for the girls. When Macci relocated his academy from the Grenelefe Resort in Haines City, Florida, to Delray Beach, Florida, the Williamses followed and settled into an estate in nearby Pompano Beach. Richard liked Macci's approach to training. The girls practiced six hours a day, six days a week; another four hours a day were spent on schoolwork. By 1993, Venus and Serena stopped attending public school and were home-schooled so they would have more time for practice. The girls trained on and off with Macci for four years, from 1991 to 1995, with a few breaks over those years to work with other coaches.

In April 1992, Venus and Serena appeared at the Family Circle Cup in Hilton Head, South Carolina. Venus was 11, and Serena was 10. The girls played an exhibition doubles match with tennis legends Billie Jean King and Rosie Casals. (Venus was paired with Casals, Serena with King.) Serena and King won the exhibition, 6-2.

Over the summer, the girls continued to train with Macci. Then Richard Williams decided to have the girls attend the Nick Bollettieri Tennis Academy (also in Florida), which is a larger training facility. Bollettieri, a renowned tennis coach who has had a huge influence in the sport, trains his players both physically and mentally and works to ensure

In this July 1992 photo, Venus Williams receives instruction from her coach Rick Macci at his training facility in Florida.

that they not only become better athletes on the court but also are better prepared to succeed off the court.

In working with Venus and Serena, Bollettieri discovered that they had excellent rotation in their hips and shoulders. In his training, Bollettieri emphasizes the importance of getting the racket head back quickly after a ground stroke; Venus and Serena mastered the skill. The sisters always approached their practices ready to play with passion and concentration; they knew how to set goals, and they kept their minds on the game. The move to Bollettieri's academy, however, lasted only six weeks. Bollettieri's staff and the Williams family had not gotten along. The Williamses soon returned to Macci's academy.

By 1993, agents were in hot pursuit of the up-and-coming tennis star Venus Williams, who would turn 14 the following year. Macci felt the decision to turn pro belonged to Richard and Oracene, but he also felt that Venus could benefit from playing tournaments at the junior level. When Richard told Macci upon his arrival in Florida in 1991 that the girls would not be playing tournaments, Macci assumed he meant for up to a year. Macci was fine with that; he felt he could work with Venus to improve her game. He had not realized that Richard would keep Venus and Serena out of competition for three years.

Richard and Oracene continued to turn down the offers. They worried about Venus turning professional too early. They wanted to give Venus and Serena a full life. They wanted equal time devoted to tennis training and education. Plus they wanted time for family fun. The pressures were intense. The question was: Could they have all that and expect the girls to reach their full potential as athletes? Only time would tell.

Going
Professional

By the winter of 1993, Venus Williams was feeling antsy. For nearly three years, she had not played competitive tennis. All of her tennis appearances had been in showcase exhibitions. She understood her parents' desire to keep her life balanced, but Venus decided to offer them a proposition. She asked her parents if she could turn professional the following summer provided she earned straight As on her school-end report card. She told her parents that she would earn the right to play professional. If Venus could hold up her end of the bargain, she hoped to make her debut at the Virginia Slims of Los Angeles tennis event.

Richard and Oracene Williams felt that it was too early for Venus to turn professional. They would never allow an agent or a coach or someone outside the family to talk them into letting Venus turn professional this early. Since the idea was coming from Venus, however, they considered it. They had raised their daughters to be responsible, thoughtful, intelligent people. In the end, Richard and Oracene decided to honor Venus's wish.

VENUS'S FIRST PROFESSIONAL MATCHES

All was going as planned. Venus received her straight-A report card, which was not difficult for her. She had worked hard at her classes, paid attention, took good notes, and studied for tests. She took schoolwork and tennis very seriously—and she took her agreement with her parents very seriously, so it was imperative that she get straight As. Venus was ready to make her professional debut.

Then, however, an incident in the tennis world scared the Williams family. Tennis star Jennifer Capriati was charged with marijuana possession. Capriati—a teen-age tennis sensation who turned professional at age 14 in 1990—had been a role model to Venus and Serena. Capriati, like Venus and Serena, had been coached by her father. Capriati, however, had become overwhelmed by the expectations she felt to win tournaments and had made some unhealthy choices. Now she decided to leave tennis altogether; she was only 18 years old.

The news rattled Venus and her family. Richard had worried about the pressures of tournaments and the media and the effect they would have on his daughters. Now he saw that he had reason to worry. Venus did, too. She no longer wanted to play the Virginia Slims tournament.

Venus's altered feelings were cemented when she and her family returned to Compton for a visit. Fans bombarded Venus, wanting to get her autograph or talk to her about what her presence on the tennis scene would mean to African Americans. It was too much for the 14-year-old

Venus. She decided she was not ready. Her parents agreed. Richard told an interviewer, "[Venus] had black people coming up to her and telling her they'd buy tickets just to see her. We told her there would be too many people expecting too much from her if she played so near her hometown. We told her, 'You can't be out there playing for the blacks, or for the whites, or whoever: it's going to be all you can do just to play for yourself when the time comes.'"[1]

In time, however, Venus regained her desire to play professionally and began to look for a tournament in which to make her debut. She found one in Oakland, California. Her parents remained unconvinced, but they respected their daughter's desire and were willing to let Venus decide. Richard and Oracene did plan to limit the number of tournaments Venus would enter, though, hoping to ease some of the pressures so many young tennis players face.

Venus wanted to turn professional sooner rather than later to take advantage of a rule the Women's Tennis Association (WTA) was set to eliminate soon. (The WTA is the organization for which Venus and Serena would play as professionals. The tournaments on the WTA Tour fall into three categories: Grand Slams, the season-ending championships, and tier-level events.) In 1994, 14-year-olds could join the WTA Tour and participate in all events. As of 1995, 14-year-olds would not be allowed to play in the Grand Slams, the season-ending championships, or the top-tier events. By 1996, 14-year-olds would not be able to play professionally at all. So if Venus turned professional in 1994, at 14, she would have the opportunity to enter any event.

Venus made her professional debut on October 31, 1994, in Oakland at the Bank of the West Classic. Everyone who followed tennis had already heard of the "Ghetto Cinderella," as her father called her. Would she prove to be as good as her father claimed? She had not had any junior

Venus Williams, 14, makes her professional debut against Shaun Stafford at the Bank of the West Classic in Oakland, California, on October 31, 1994.

tennis experience in the past three years. The day before the tournament, Venus's father took her to Disneyland. He wanted her to remember to enjoy life and not take the tournament too seriously. But would Venus take the tournament seriously *enough*?

Venus did not disappoint. She proved her talent and her commitment when she stepped onto the court and put everything into the match. Her energy and concentration excited the crowd. Her powerful serves and her swift movement around the court demonstrated her impressive athleticism. Venus faced Shaun Stafford, the fifty-ninth-ranked player in the world; Venus beat her in two sets, 6-3, 6-4. In her next match, Venus faced the No. 2-ranked player in the world, Arantxa Sánchez-Vicario. Although Venus won the first set, Sánchez-Vicario came back to beat the young rising star in three sets.

Regardless of the loss, Venus was happy to have been a part of the Bank of the West Classic and proved to the tennis world that she belonged. After the match, she grabbed a microphone and thanked the crowd for making her first tennis tournament so much fun. She earned $5,400 in her first professional event.

True to his word, Richard did not allow Venus to participate in many tournaments. In fact, the Bank of the West Classic was her only tournament in 1994. Still, by May 1995, Venus had already signed a five-year, multimillion-dollar contract with Reebok. She had played in only one pro tournament to date. Reebok, however, believed Venus would turn into a champion. Along with Venus's deal, Richard received a consultant's salary with Reebok, which allowed the family to move to a 10-acre estate near West Palm Beach, Florida, complete with its own tennis courts.

Venus's second professional tournament came in August 1995 at the Acura Classic in Los Angeles, California. Venus, tall and gangly, wearing white beads in her hair and a white silk vest, looked the part but played poorly. In the first round, she faced Asa Carlsson, who easily beat her.

The next week, Venus played in her third tournament, this time in Canada. Venus faced thirty-third-ranked Sabine Appelmans. Rain delayed the match for two hours. Venus lost but played well. She was a good sport about the loss and told an interviewer afterward that she was doing the best she could and was happy for the experience. Venus also told the interviewer that she was working on her slice and her inside game. Also present at the Canadian tournament was another teenage sensation, Martina Hingis. She, like Venus, was born in 1980 and entered the pros at 14. Already ranked twenty-first in the world, Hingis won two matches at the tournament before losing in the third round.

The next year, Venus returned to the Acura Classic in Los Angeles. She made it to the third round, where she faced the world's No. 1 player, Steffi Graf of Germany. Although Venus played well, she lost the match, 6-4, 6-4. In 1996, Venus played in only six events; in four of those tournaments, she lost in the first round. She could have played in many others—the public wanted to see more of Venus. It was unusual for a professional to play in so few tournaments. In fact, Venus had begun to develop a mystique, because the public saw so little of her. Even the other players on the tour did not know what to think of her. Venus came across as aloof and not part of the group. Yet even though the public hoped to see Venus play in more tournaments, Richard would not allow it. He wanted to make sure his daughters' education came first and insisted that they get not only As, but A+s on their report cards. Richard had every intention of ensuring that Venus and Serena were prepared for what was to come after tennis.

Venus made her 1997 debut in March at the State Farm Evert Cup in Indian Wells, California. She arrived with a new beaded hairdo featuring red, white, and blue beads— 1,800 beads that took 10 hours to put in. In the second round, Venus lost the first set to Ai Sugiyama, but she did not allow herself to lose confidence. During the first set, she learned that Sugiyama's forehand was weaker than her backhand, so Venus began to hit to her forehand. With the change in her game, Venus won the next two sets and the match. To get into the quarterfinals, Venus defeated ninth-ranked Iva Majoli in a close, three-set match that lasted more than two-and-a-half hours. Majoli told interviewers after the match, "[Venus's] first serve is very, very strong, and once she puts her first serve in, it's almost 100 percent her point."[2] In the quarterfinals, Venus lost to Lindsay Davenport, the tournament's eventual champion.

In April 1997, Venus entered the Bausch & Lomb Championships, which is played on a clay court. Tennis tournaments are played on clay courts, hard courts, grass courts, or indoors. Venus lost in the second round to Chanda Rubin. Rubin forced Venus to move around the clay court, which Venus did not find easy. Clay courts can be more difficult for power players like Venus, because the clay slows down the ball. Venus said later that she thought that hard courts better suited her game.

VENUS TAKES ON THE GRAND SLAMS

The first Grand Slam tournament that Venus entered was the 1997 French Open, held in Paris. The clay-court tournament takes place at Stade de Roland Garros, located near a beautiful park. Venus, who had studied French in school, packed up her French books and was ready to try out her French-speaking skills. On her first trip outside the United States, Venus traveled with her mother and sister Serena. Richard stayed home. He did not want to become a courtside parent, and Venus understood his decision. Venus was in France with a specific goal in mind: to win her first Slam.

When ninetieth-ranked Venus took to the court in a shiny silver outfit and a head full of jangling white beads, the French audience—intrigued by her sense of style— watched with interest. They soon discovered there was more to Venus than her appearance; she played tennis with determination, confidence, and joy. They watched as she took on forty-fifth-ranked Naoko Sawamatsu in the first round and proceeded to win a competitive match.

Between matches, Venus stayed close to Oracene and Serena. Oracene doubled as a coach, so she was able to give Venus notes on her game. And Serena was not only Venus's sister but also her best friend. Oracene and Serena were Venus's support group, the people who believed in her. Together, they brought one another strength.

Venus's strong support group and her belief in herself, however, were not enough. Venus found herself in trouble in the second round, losing to Nathalie Tauziat in three sets. Venus, who had expected to win, was sad about the loss, knowing that she had not played her best. But she would overcome the loss. Venus believed in maintaining a winning mentality, so she put the French Open behind her and looked forward to her next Grand Slam: Wimbledon.

Venus headed to England to prepare for her first Wimbledon, the very place her father had declared she would win a title one day. Venus had just celebrated her seventeenth birthday. She arrived in England with purple and green beads covering her braids. Although eager to play in her second Slam, she did not make it past the first round, losing to ninety-first-ranked Magdalena Grzybowska.

Then it was on to the U.S. Open. Once again, Venus was eager to get on the court. She felt ready to prove that she could advance further in a Slam. Venus was earning a reputation among the other players because of her tendency to keep her distance from them and her confidence in her ability to become No. 1. Her competitors saw her demeanor as standoffish and intimidating. Although no one was talking directly to Venus, many players were talking *about* her. Venus wanted no part of the gossip. She paid no attention to what other players thought of her. She focused her attention on the game.

The unseeded Venus, ranked sixty-sixth in the world, won her first two matches. In the third round, nearly 22,000 people watched from the stands as Venus easily defeated the eighth seed, Anke Huber, in a huge upset. Now, as Venus began to push her way through the rounds at the U.S. Open, players not only found her intimidating *off* the court but *on* the court as well. Players began to dread playing her. In the quarterfinals, Venus beat seventeenth-ranked Sandrine Testud to ensure her first spot ever in a Grand Slam semifinal.

Her opponent was Irina Spîrlea of Romania, who was the eleventh seed in the tournament. Spîrlea, six years older than Venus, had turned pro in 1990, when she was 16. In an unusually long, two-hour-forty-two-minute, three-set match that included two tiebreakers, Venus did what she had set out to do: She earned herself a spot in the U.S. Open finals. The match displayed Venus's ability to keep the pressure on her opponent. She kept her head up, kept her feet moving, and kept chasing and returning balls. She never gave up or backed down.

The match between Venus and Spîrlea made the news for more than just tennis, however. During a second-set changeover (when players trade sides of the court on which they play), the two women bumped into each other. Venus did not even look at Spîrlea, who seemed to be trying to force eye contact. Instead of looking at her opponent, Venus headed to her bench and started to study her notes; she was done with the incident. Venus later found out that Spîrlea, on the other hand, was making a fuss about it on her end of the court, smirking and laughing to friends, family, and fans in the stands. Reporters made much of the incident, replaying the run-in on television as well as writing about it. They also focused on how the two women handled the situation. Spîrlea's attitude made her look immature, and she received bad press. Venus knew that she was just as responsible for the collision, as neither of them had stepped aside. Venus, though, was happy with herself for maintaining her composure and putting the incident aside to focus on what was important—the game.

Richard was not as good a sport as Venus was. Richard, who saw the bump on television from the family's home in Florida, thought it was intentional on Spîrlea's part, possibly with racial connotations. He publicly referred to Spîrlea as a "big white turkey."[3] Within a couple of months, Richard retracted his accusations and said he had blown the incident out of proportion.

Despite these tensions, Venus had accomplished something phenomenal that day and was not about to let any controversy taint her achievements: She had become the first black woman to reach the U.S. Open final since Althea Gibson won the 1958 championship. She was also the first unseeded woman to reach the U.S. Open final since Darlene Hard faced Gibson in 1958.

In the finals, Venus faced her peer Martina Hingis. Three-and-a-half months younger than Venus, Hingis—like Venus—was raised to become a tennis champion. And Hingis had already proved that she was a star. Going into the final, Hingis was ranked No. 1 in the world. She had won the Australian Open and Wimbledon that year. She was the runner-up at the French Open. And Hingis would take home the U.S. Open, easily defeating Venus, 6-0, 6-4.

After Venus's spectacular run in New York, the Williams family returned to their home in Florida. They spent their days practicing and training. Richard started to post signs around the property to remind Venus and Serena of important lessons. For example, one sign read, "Serena: You must learn to listen."[4] Another read, "Serena: You must learn to use more topspin on the ball."[5] For Venus, Richard posted, "Venus: You must take control of your future."[6] And another read, "Venus: When you fail, you fail alone."[7] The girls channeled these words of advice into motivation to strive toward and reach their dreams: winning tennis championships.

SERENA'S FIRST PROFESSIONAL MATCHES

Richard often described Serena as the one who would eventually pass Venus. He felt that Serena had more power and talent than Venus. She was hard hitting and fearless. In October 1995, Serena Williams, then 14, was ready to turn professional. With the WTA's new rules in place, 14-year-olds were not allowed to play in the major events. So Serena's opening debut was far less flashy than Venus's had been. Serena was allowed to play on the basis of her celebrity (which at this point came from being the daughter of Richard Williams and the sister of Venus Williams) in the Bell Challenge in Quebec, Canada. Serena faced Anne Miller and lost quickly in a match dominated by Miller.

ALTHEA GIBSON

Althea Gibson was born on August 25, 1927. Using her signature serve-and-volley style of play, she became the first prominent African-American tennis champion. With her tall frame (5 feet 10 inches, or 178 centimeters) and lean body, Gibson had the physique of a power player.

On July 4, 1957, Gibson won the first of two consecutive Wimbledon singles titles. In 1957, she beat Christine Truman in a commanding victory in the semifinals and then defeated Darlene Hard to win the final. In 1958, she took out Britain's Angela Mortimer Barrett in the Wimbledon finals. Besides the two Wimbledon wins, Gibson captured the French title in 1956 and two United States titles (1957 and 1958).

In Gibson's day, the players were amateurs and did not receive prize money. After her U.S. championship win in 1958, Gibson retired from amateur tennis and began to play on exhibition tours to earn money. Gibson died in 2003 at the age of 76.

Early in their careers, well before Venus's run to the U.S. Open final, the tennis world buzzed about the Williams sisters: Was it a mistake that they had played in so few tournaments before turning pro? Was their father all hype and empty talk about these tennis sensations? After all, Serena had failed to impress in her debut. When interviewed after the match, though, Serena made it known that she was not backing down. She told the *New York Times*, "I feel like I'm more ready than ever to get out here and compete with the professionals. Once I make a decision, I never go back on it."[8]

Like Venus, Serena did not play many tournaments in her first years as a professional. Unlike Venus, Serena was unable to play in the larger tournaments. But she accompanied Venus to those events. As she supported her sister from the sidelines, she learned the ins and outs of various players and deepened her knowledge of the game.

In November 1997, Serena entered the Ameritech Cup in Chicago, Illinois. Here, she faced off against Mary Pierce, the seventh-ranked player in the world. Serena, ranked 304th, stunned the crowd by beating Pierce in two sets. Serena was in the quarterfinals, where she met Monica Seles, the fourth-ranked player in the world. Although Serena lost the first set, she fought back and won the next two. Serena had won the match, 4-6, 6-1, 6-1; she told interviewers afterward that, when she was little, she had always wanted to play Seles. Serena became the lowest-ranked player ever to defeat two top-10 players in the same tournament. In her first career semifinal, Serena lost to Lindsay Davenport. With her success at the Ameritech Cup, however, Serena's ranking in the WTA took an amazing jump—from 304 to 102!

Later in November, Serena jammed her left wrist in a skateboarding accident. The injury forced Serena to ease up on her two-handed backhand; instead, she developed

On November 6, 1997, Serena Williams hits a return on her way to upsetting seventh-ranked Mary Pierce in the second round of the Ameritech Cup in Chicago. Williams wins 6-3, 7-6 (7-3).

a commanding forehand. Serena would use this forehand when she and Venus traveled to Sydney, Australia, for the Sydney International tournament in January 1998. There, the sisters made it through to the semifinals. In her match, Venus knocked out Ai Sugiyama to get into the finals.

Serena, however, fell to Arantxa Sánchez-Vicario. Had she won, Serena would have faced Venus in the finals. Instead, Venus took on Sánchez-Vicario, who played a consistent game and won the match.

Next up was the 1998 Australian Open, the first of the year's four Grand Slams and Serena's first ever. In the first round, Venus faced Alexia Dechaume-Balleret and Serena faced Irina Spîrlea, who was the sixth seed; the sisters prevailed. In the second round, each would face an opponent she knew very well—her sister. This marked the first time the sisters played against each other as professionals. Venus won, despite a close first set, 7-6, 6-1. Although Venus did not feel badly about *winning*, she *did* feel badly about defeating her younger sister; she wished, too, that the match had been a final.

Venus beat Amélie Mauresmo and Patty Schnyder to make her way to the quarterfinals. Here Venus faced Lindsay Davenport. Although Venus won the first set, Davenport came back to take the match. Venus, who believes she can learn from every loss, told reporters afterward that she needed to capitalize on her opportunities. She believed she had not taken advantage of the chances she had against Davenport, but she knew she would next time. Despite the loss, Venus did not leave the Australian Open empty-handed. She and her partner Justin Gimelstob took home the mixed-doubles title.

THE PERSONALITIES OF VENUS AND SERENA

As the sisters grew in popularity, it became clear that Venus and Serena were very different tennis players—and very different people. Venus serves big nearly all the time. She has become known for serving balls at speeds greater than 125 miles an hour (201 kilometers per hour). She depends on her serve and her overhead smash to help her win games. Venus likes to hit deep. Serena, on the other hand, mixes up

Serena, left, Oracene, and Venus Williams pose for the media during the Lipton Championships in Key Biscayne, Florida, on March 20, 1999.

her serves a bit more and sometimes goes for precise placement of the ball, rather than simply a big serve. Serena has one of the most powerful backhands in tennis. Both Venus and Serena play with an attacking style that has become more popular because of them.

The sisters play with great confidence and determination—they believe they can do what they set out to do. Venus told interviewer Anjali Rao, when asked if she ever doubts herself, "No, I think everyone has moments of doubt, but for me, I think I know that I've put the time in on the court or whatever that I'm pursuing. I'm this over-achiever type, I'll just work and work and I'll just do it over and over and over again. And I know I spent the time and I have the confidence. You know, anytime that I try something new, I just work at it and that builds confidence."9 The sisters' willingness to set goals and practice has allowed them to excel in many areas.

Venus is quieter, while Serena is more outgoing. Venus keeps mostly to herself, while Serena enjoys talking to people—even those she does not know very well. Venus invests much of her money, while Serena is a free spender. Venus finds learning about new cultures and cities exciting. She spends time in art museums, antique shops, and markets when she visits a new place. She is intrigued by new foods—especially Thai, Indian, and Greek—and would like to have time to try cooking some of the exotic foods she has tasted. Serena is drawn to acting, even though it sometimes makes her nervous. But she enjoys the challenge of trying something out of her comfort zone.

Both sisters spend hours reading, learning languages (among them French and Spanish), watching HGTV (Home & Garden Television), and listening to music (they both like Green Day). They also love to travel, play guitar, and design. They have their differences, too. Venus loves New York and London, while Serena loves Los Angeles. Venus plays an acoustic guitar, while Serena plays electric. Venus studies all kinds of design (including architecture, home décor, and jewelry), while Serena prefers fashion.

Venus and Serena spent nearly all of their time together as children. As they have gotten older, they have remained best friends. Even when they are at different tournaments, they stay in touch by e-mail or text messages. Though at one time Serena wanted to do whatever Venus was doing, she has blossomed into her own person, and the two sisters now appreciate each other for both their similarities and their differences.

Rising in
the Ranks

Besides improving their games, Venus and Serena Williams were working hard on their educations. In January 1998, Venus graduated from the Driftwood Academy, a private school in Lake Park, Florida. Serena graduated the following August; around the same time she signed a five-year, multimillion-dollar deal with Puma.

On the court, the sisters were starting to win more. In March 1998, Venus captured her first professional title at the IGA Tennis Classic in Oklahoma City. After an unexpected win against Lindsay Davenport in the semifinals, Venus faced Joannette Kruger to win the title. Venus took home $27,000 for her win. Venus and Serena had also begun to play doubles together and won their first title in Oklahoma City.

GAINING EXPERIENCE ON THE COURTS

At the State Farm Evert Cup later that month, Venus again faced Martina Hingis, the teenage sensation who was now a four-time Grand Slam title winner. On a chilly spring afternoon, with a light raining falling, Venus and Hingis played competitively in the semifinals. Hingis, in this case, came out the winner and went on to take the title.

Just a few weeks later, Venus had another opportunity to beat Hingis—at the 1998 Lipton Championships semifinals in Key Biscayne, Florida. To get to the semifinals, Hingis had beaten Serena by saving a pair of match points in a close contest. Venus was ready for her turn against Hingis. After an hour and fifty-eight minutes of intense tennis, Venus came out on top. In the final, 17-year-old Venus squared off against 16-year-old Anna Kournikova. Venus lost the first set but came back strong to take control of the match and win. This important top-tier championship crown came with $250,000 in prize money.

In May, Venus and Serena flew to Italy to play in the Italian Open. Oracene proudly watched each of her daughters win matches that took place at the same time, but she had to run back and forth between courts to keep abreast of the scores! Venus beat Alexandra Fusai, while Serena defeated Conchita Martínez.

Venus's and Serena's wins meant a second sister-sister duel at the professional level—this time in the Italian Open quarterfinals. Venus took the win in a match in which both sisters committed numerous unforced errors and double faults. The fans and the press were beginning to grumble about Venus and Serena playing each other. Some people felt the sisters did not play hard enough against each other. They thought the sisters were holding back, as if to protect the other from having to lose. Venus and Serena dismissed the talk. They said their purpose was to win any match, regardless of who was on the other side of the net.

Venus, despite a sore left knee, went on to beat Arantxa Sánchez-Vicario in the semifinals. Venus was matched against Hingis again in the final. This time, however, Hingis would take the title. At the ceremony after Hingis's win, Hingis and Venus were gracious and friendly to the crowd. Venus told the onlookers, "Every day the sun shined, Rome got more beautiful. I don't think I would mind moving here."[1] When a man yelled back in Italian, "You can come to my house," Venus, after hearing the translation, replied jokingly, "Tell him that he can have Serena."[2]

Venus lost again to Hingis in the quarterfinals of the French Open in June. Venus did, however, take home a second mixed-doubles title along with partner Justin Gimelstob. They defeated Serena and her partner Luis Lobo in the finals.

In June 1998, the Williams family traveled to England to play at Wimbledon. Just before the tournament, Serena had reached the quarterfinals of the Direct Line Insurance Championships in Eastbourne, England. Advancing to the quarterfinals had made Serena one of the fastest-rising players ever on the WTA Tour. She now ranked in the top 20.

During a warm-up tournament on her eighteenth birthday, Venus was beaten by Natasha Zvereva. Once Wimbledon began, however, Venus turned on her game. She reached the quarterfinals by defeating Virginia Ruano Pascual, who had gotten by Serena in the previous round when Serena bowed out with a strained left calf muscle. In defaulting, Serena ended any chance of taking the singles title in her Wimbledon debut. Serena did, however, win the mixed-doubles title with her partner Max Mirnyi. In Venus's quarterfinal round, she lost a close match to Jana Novotna.

At the 1998 U.S. Open, both Venus and Serena had their sights on winning the championship. Serena, at her first U.S. Open, was taken out early, though, when she lost to Irina Spîrlea in the third round. If a Williams sister was going to win the U.S. Open singles title *this* year, Venus would have to do it. Before the competition, Venus had asked Reebok to design seven tennis outfits for her so that she would have a new one for each round of the tournament.

In her opening round against Elena Wagner, Venus wore a navy-and-gold sleeveless outfit. She easily defeated Wagner. When Venus faced Mary Pierce in the fourth round, she had to deal with a rain delay. Venus rose to the challenge, although she had to win the second set in a tiebreak. In the quarterfinal, Venus beat Arantxa Sánchez-Vicario by attacking and anticipating the ball. Venus felt ready for her sixth match of the tournament, during which she would wear a red outfit with the back cut out. Unfortunately, there would be no seventh appearance. In the semifinals, Venus lost to Lindsay Davenport.

Serena and her partner Max Mirnyi took home another mixed-doubles title at the 1998 U.S. Open, when they beat Lisa Raymond and Pat Galbraith. Between Venus and Serena and their partners Justin Gimelstob and Max Mirnyi, the Williams sisters had a Grand Slam sweep in mixed doubles in 1998.

Venus did not sit still for long after the U.S. Open. The following month she was on a plane to Zurich, Switzerland, where she played in the European Championships. In her quarterfinal match against Pierce, Venus blasted a 127-mile-an-hour (204-kilometer-per-hour) serve that Pierce could not return. Venus's previous record had been 125 miles an hour (201 kilometers per hour) at Wimbledon. Venus played a powerful, aggressive match—the kind for which she was becoming known and feared—in defeating Pierce.

Venus continued her aggressive play to make it to the final against Lindsay Davenport—again. Once again, however, Davenport was the better player on this day and took home the title and $1 million in prize money.

Venus hoped to end the year by playing in her first Chase Championships at Madison Square Garden in New York, an event in which only the top 16 players in the world were eligible to play. Venus, though, would have to postpone her Chase debut: She was suffering tendinitis in her left knee. The sisters ended the year by writing, designing, and editing a newsletter called the *Tennis Monthly Recap*, which they distributed the following month at the Australian Open.

SISTER AGAINST SISTER

Venus started 1999 ranked No. 5, and Serena started the year ranked No. 21. Richard felt that his daughters were in a position to rack up titles and get closer to becoming the top two players in the world. He worried about what it would do to their psyches, however, if they had to face each other for a title. He decided to avoid this by not having Venus and Serena enter the same non-Grand Slam events.

The Australian Open proved to be disappointing for the Williams sisters. Serena fell in the third round to the fourteenth seed, Sandrine Testud. Venus made it all the way to the quarterfinals, where she lost to Lindsay Davenport. Much of Venus's troubles started in the second set, when the umpire called a let after a string of beads from Venus's hair broke and fell onto the court. (When a let is called, the point is replayed.) The umpire told Venus that if it happened again, she would lose a point. Again some beads fell out, and the umpire called point. An upset Venus challenged the call, but the tournament referee agreed with the umpire. The call stood. Unable to regain her concentration after that, she played poorly. When asked after the match if she would change her hairstyle, Venus said: "I like my hair."[3]

In February 1999, Venus got another chance to win a title when she played in the final of the IGA Tennis Classic in Oklahoma City. On the same day, Serena was busy taking

GRAND SLAMS

In tennis, there are four major events each year—the Australian Open, the French Open, Wimbledon, and the U.S. Open. A singles player or a doubles team who win all four championships in the same calendar year has achieved the Grand Slam.

The Australian Open, held in January, is the first tournament of the calendar year. It is played in downtown Melbourne at the National Tennis Center at Flinders Park. The tournament is played on hard courts, and the two main courts have a retractable roof, which ends the need for rain delays and protects players from mercilessly high temperatures, for which Melbourne is known at that time of year.

The French Open takes place in late spring in Paris, France, at Stade de Roland Garros. The players compete on red clay courts. Then Wimbledon, played on grass courts, takes place in London in late June/early July at the All England Lawn Tennis Club. The final event, the U.S. Open, is held in late August/early September at the Billie Jean King National Tennis Center at Flushing Meadows-Corona Park in Queens, New York City. The U.S. Open is played on hard courts.

The four major tournaments last two weeks each. To win the tournament, a player or doubles team must make it through seven rounds. People refer to "needing to peak" at the right time for a victory. Tennis players try to hold back in early rounds and then let their best play come out at the right time to take home a Grand Slam title.

part in her own final across the globe at the Open Gaz de France tournament in Paris. Serena won the title—her first on the WTA Tour—over Amélie Mauresmo in a competitive, three-set match. Although Venus was not able to speak to Serena, she heard about her sister's win from their father. About five hours after Serena's victory, Venus began her final against Amanda Coetzer, handily winning the match. Venus and Serena became the first sisters ever to win separate titles in the same week.

In March 1999, Serena played at the Evert Cup in Indian Wells, California. She came out strong to beat second-ranked Lindsay Davenport in the second round, eighth-ranked Mary Pierce in the quarterfinals, and seventh-ranked Steffi Graf in the finals. She earned $200,000 for her title. Serena had now gone 11 matches without losing. The Williams sisters were on a roll.

Although it would mean a possible showdown between sisters, Venus and Serena entered the Lipton Championships later in March. Serena ensured herself a spot in the finals when she defeated the world's top-ranked player, Martina Hingis, in two sets. With her win over Hingis, Serena had now gone undefeated in 16 straight matches. Venus also earned a spot in the finals when she dominated her semifinal against Graf. It would be sister against sister for the title. The last time two sisters had played for a major title was in 1884 at Wimbledon when 19-year-old Maud Watson defeated her 26-year-old sister, Lillian.

When Venus and Serena faced off in the Lipton final, their father was in the stands. He had a grease pencil and a hand-held message board on which he wrote seven messages throughout the match and held them up for television cameras to see. (Venus said she could not see the message board from the courts.) The first message Richard showed the world read, "Welcome to the Williams Show."[4] The second sign, referring to his claim that his daughters would

Serena Williams celebrates her upset victory over Monica Seles at the U.S. Open tennis tournament in New York on September 8, 1999. Williams beats Seles 4-6, 6-3, 6-2.

one day become No. 1 and No. 2, read, "I told you so!"[5] When Venus defeated Serena in the first set, Richard's third sign read, "Go Serena Go!"[6] During the second set, when Serena started to show more power, Richard held up a sign that read, "It Couldn't Have Happened to a Better Family."[7] Richard took a cigarette break and returned at the start of the third set, after Serena had won the second. Richard held up a fifth sign that read, "Hello to My Mother-in-Law, Ora Lee Price,"[8] and soon after another sign read, "Hello to My Friends in Compton."[9] Getting off topic, Richard then held up a final sign that read, "The Williams Family Loves Fox TV."[10] Soon after, Serena lost the match to Venus, 6-1, 4-6, 6-4.

The sisters were subdued following the match; Venus did not celebrate with her usual display of giddiness and dancing. Along with their crystal bowl trophies, Venus collected $265,000 for her title and Serena took home $132,000 as runner-up. Despite the loss, Serena had become the ninth-ranked player in the world.

Following her Lipton title, Venus took part in the Betty Barclay Cup in Hamburg, Germany. The tournament was held on a clay court, and Venus had yet to win a title on clay. Venus made it past the semifinals when she easily beat Arantxa Sánchez-Vicario. In the final, Venus shut down Mary Pierce in a one-sided performance. Venus had now won five career titles, including one on clay. She earned $80,000 in winning the tournament.

Both Venus and Serena entered the 1999 Italian Open in May. In the third round, Venus beat Gala León García, although she had a hard time pulling out the win. Serena, on the other hand, easily beat Tatiana Panova. In the next round, both sisters played aggressively and took out two competitive players. Serena played first, beating Irina Spîrlea. Then she took the stands to watch Venus defeat Anna Kournikova. Next, in the quarterfinals, Serena fell to Martina Hingis, while Venus defeated Dominique Van Roost. The semifinals had a familiar lineup: Venus Williams and Hingis—the two had played each other in the final at the 1998 Italian Open. This time, however, Venus was the victor.

In the final, Venus pulled out a victory over Pierce to win the Italian Open. A smiling Venus told the crowd after accepting her trophy, "I have a lot of dreams, and most of them come true these days."[11] Venus played an aggressive game, serving 12 aces and hitting 19 winners. She made only 11 unforced errors.

Serena and Oracene left the Italian Open to head for Germany, where Serena played in Berlin. She ended up retiring from the tournament with an arm injury. Venus, meanwhile, flew back to Florida to practice for the French Open. With her success that spring on clay courts, Venus hoped that the French Open would be her first Slam title. Instead, she lost in three sets in a fourth-round upset to 125th-ranked Barbara Schwartz. Schwartz's win shocked Venus, who had not scouted her opponent ahead of time; Venus had assumed that Schwartz was the one who needed to worry about Venus's game. Instead, Schwartz's one-handed backhand slice caught Venus off-guard and cost her the match. Serena, too, lost in an early round to Mary Joe Fernandez. Venus and Serena did manage much better in the doubles event at the French Open, winning the title over Martina Hingis and Anna Kournikova.

In August, each sister took home a singles title. In the semifinals of the Pilot Pen tournament in Connecticut, Venus beat Monica Seles using her 125-mile-an-hour serve. In the final, Venus defeated Lindsay Davenport; that win moved Venus to No. 3 in the rankings. Serena's title came at the Acura Classic in Manhattan Beach, California. She defeated Martina Hingis in the semifinals and Julie Halard-Decugis in the finals to capture her first singles title since March.

FIRST GRAND SLAM WIN

The previous year, Venus had helped Reebok design seven tennis outfits—one for each round of the U.S. Open. She never had a chance to wear the seventh. Now, Venus hoped to wear seven all-new outfits that she and Reebok came up with for the tournament. Venus had created one of them, a one-shoulder design, herself.

In the quarterfinals, Serena, who was seeded seventh, made a strong comeback from a set down to defeat Monica Seles in three sets. Both Serena and Venus, who was seeded third, made it into the semifinals. Each of their matches went to three sets. Serena took down Lindsay Davenport, but Venus lost to the top seed, Hingis. Serena, in her first Grand Slam final, would take on Hingis.

Serena gave it her all, served with power, and won the tiebreaker in the second set to take the match, 6-3, 7-6. Two weeks shy of her eighteenth birthday, Serena became the first Williams sister to capture a Grand Slam title.

IN HER OWN WORDS

Venus Williams often reflects on the path her life has taken. She once said:

> It's been a journey. For women of color, for my family. It's one dream coming true after another.

Althea Gibson, the first African American to win the U.S. Championships (the forerunner to the U.S. Open), congratulated Serena on her accomplishment. It had been 41 years since an African-American woman (Gibson) had won any Grand Slam. President Bill Clinton and his daughter, Chelsea, also congratulated Serena by telephone. Serena was awarded $750,000 for her win.

During her match against Hingis, Serena looked toward Venus, who was sitting in the family box, for emotional support. "I saw Venus over there really making sure, pumping me up; it really helped me," Serena said.[12]

DID YOU KNOW?

The Williams sisters have helped to revolutionize the tennis world. Before they came on the scene, tennis was primarily a sport for white, upper-class players; African-American tennis stars were rare. They also changed the way tennis is played. Women's tennis had primarily been a gentler, more refined game. Like Martina Navratilova before them, Venus and Serena showed the world that it was all right for women to have muscle and play tennis with power and speed. At first, some people criticized their muscular bodies, saying women should play a "feminine" game of tennis. But young girls making their way in the junior circuits now know that being fit, strong, and muscular is necessary.

Before Venus and Serena brought boldly colored outfits and hairstyles to the sport, tennis outfits for women tended to be simple, traditional white apparel, and hair was tied back in a ponytail or cut short. Venus stormed onto the tennis scene wearing solid, bright colors that matched her energy and speed. At the 2000 U.S. Open, Serena, in an early round, wore a black Puma mesh outfit complete with a fuchsia-colored tie-dyed print

The next day, Serena and Venus teamed up to play in the doubles final. The sisters defeated Chanda Rubin and Sandrine Testud in three sets. The last time sisters had won the U.S. Open had been more than 100 years earlier, when Juliette and Kathleen Atkinson had won in 1897 and 1898. This was Venus and Serena's second Grand Slam doubles title.

BALANCING TENNIS AND OUTSIDE LIVES

In October, Venus and Serena traveled to Munich, Germany, to play in the Grand Slam Cup. Both sisters made it

and tennis shoes to match. In 2004, Nike designed knee-high tennis boots for Serena.

The sisters' hairstyles have also changed over the years. They both started their careers with braided hair covered in colored beads that they would change depending on where they were playing—red, white, and blue for the U.S. Open; all white for Wimbledon. In the early 2000s, Serena bleached her hair and wore it braided and tied back in a ponytail.

David N. Dinkins, the former mayor of New York City, told the *New York Times*, "[Venus and Serena] have done for tennis, to some degree at least, that which Tiger Woods did for golf. People who before had no interest in the sport, now have it. I think [Venus and Serena] clearly have an appeal. Go back to when they dared to be different. They were wearing beads. They have such confidence in their own ability." *

---

*Liz Robbins, "Noticed: Williams mania Sweeps the Black A-List." *New York Times*. September 9, 2001.

to the semifinals, where each won her matches. Venus beat Martina Hingis, and Serena beat Lindsay Davenport. In the final, which went to three sets, it was Serena who was victorious, winning 6-1, 3-6, 6-3. After the match, Venus gave her little sister a hug at the net to congratulate her.

During 1999, Serena suffered frequent injuries that forced her to withdraw from competitions. She was unable to play in Hilton Head because of patella tendinitis in her right knee, and she pulled out of her quarterfinal match in the German Open with a strained right elbow. She was forced to withdraw from Wimbledon before the tournament had begun because of influenza and a back injury. She then had to withdraw from the Chase Championships because of a strained back. Even though Serena played infrequently in 1999, she ended the year ranked No. 4 in the world. Venus finished the year one spot ahead, at No. 3.

The sisters were busy off the court, too. Venus and Serena participated in an automobile-safety campaign in November, filming a public-service announcement promoting seat-belt use. To get the message out about seat-belt safety (car accidents were the No. 1 killer of teenagers in America), the sisters told their audience: "Tennis is a game; life is not: buckle up."[13] Richard and Oracene appeared in the commercial, too.

Venus and Serena also started college at the Art Institute of Fort Lauderdale. The sisters had always had a passion for design and wanted to develop their creative talents. When Venus was eight years old, her mother had given her a sewing machine. Oracene was an avid seamstress and loved to make clothing for her daughters. Venus used the sewing machine to make clothes for her Barbie dolls, though she admits to not having been a good seamstress. Design school gave Venus and Serena another way to channel their talents.

At the start of 2000, Venus and Serena continued to struggle with health problems. At the Australian Open in January, Serena was troubled by a back injury in her first-round match and lost in the fourth round to Elena Likhovtseva. Venus was unable to play in the Australian Open because of tendinitis in both wrists. When Venus decided not to play in the Ericsson Open in Key Biscayne, Florida, in March, people began to wonder if she was going to retire.

Meanwhile, Serena had made it to the final of the Open Gaz de France in early February. During the match against Nathalie Tauziat, she injured a ligament in her right knee in the sixth game of the first set. She was hampered for the rest of the match, which Tauziat won. A week later, Serena captured the Faber Grand Prix title in Hanover, Germany. A month and a half later, at the Amelia Island tournament, Serena was forced to withdraw because of a meniscus tear in her left foot. Later in the summer, Serena beat Hingis and then Davenport to take the Los Angeles title. But the following week, at the Canadian Open, she had to retire in the final against Hingis when the base of her left foot became inflamed.

Serena also withdrew from the Family Circle Cup in Hilton Head, South Carolina. This time, it was not for health reasons. She joined the National Association for the Advancement of Colored People's boycott of South Carolina for flying the Confederate flag over its statehouse.

Around this time, Venus (then 19) and Serena (then 18) purchased a new home just around the corner from their parents' house. They wanted to be near their family but also wanted more freedom from their parents. While they saw their parents often and enjoyed being with them, the move allowed them to feel more grown-up and independent.

THE 2000 WIMBLEDON WIN

Serena also had to withdraw from the French Open because of a knee injury, so by the time Wimbledon came around, she was itching to get back into competitive play. (Venus had finally gotten over her wrist injury and had made it to the quarterfinals of the French Open.) During Wimbledon, both sisters played hard, and their games were sharp and powerful. In the quarterfinals, Venus faced Martina Hingis, and Serena faced Lisa Raymond. Serena dominated Raymond, winning in just 41 minutes. The question remained: Would she face Hingis or her sister in the Wimbledon semifinal?

Venus's quarterfinal against Martina Hingis took three sets. The winner's final serve was a 118-mile-an-hour (190-kilometer-per-hour) ace. The server was Venus Williams. A sister-sister semifinal would occur.

Venus had worked very hard to get there, overcoming numerous injuries. Over the years, she had put in long hours toward her dream of winning at Wimbledon. The year 2000 felt like the time to do just that. She later wrote in *Serving from the Hip*: "When I arrived at Wimbledon that year [2000], I felt like I had no choice but to win. I had been practicing very hard, I had been playing well, and I felt I deserved it."[14]

Tennis fans and the press were eager to see the outcome of the semifinal between Venus and Serena. The media, hoping for an even more exciting story, tried hard to uncover feelings of animosity or jealousy between the sisters. Venus had yet to win a Grand Slam. Would this match be Venus's revenge for Serena having won the family's first Slam? When reporters asked Venus about the semifinal match, she said, "I see it as an opportunity, not as an opportunity against Serena."[15] Richard tried to explain to reporters, "I think [Venus and Serena are] excited to get this far, but you have to understand human feelings. I don't think they're excited about playing each other, but their family bond is stronger than tennis."[16]

That bond would be tested when Venus and Serena stepped onto Centre Court at the All England Lawn Tennis

Club. Neither parent watched the match in person. Richard was too nervous and spent his time walking the grounds at the club. Oracene was back in Florida, exhausted from the publicity leading up to the match. She preferred to watch it unfold on television at home, where she would have her privacy. Although Richard and Oracene were not on the sidelines, they were still with their daughters. They were supporting their every move.

The tension on the court was apparent, and the crowd seemed unsure about whom to cheer for—it was unusually quiet in the stands. Venus and Serena both made more errors than usual and did not seem comfortable on the court. Watching them play, it was apparent how well each sister knew the other. They both seemed able to predict where the other would serve, and the speed and athleticism with which they got to the ball time and time again were breathtaking. Still, neither one appeared fully relaxed. Although Venus maintained her usual composure, she also looked somewhat nervous. Serena was more animated, slapping her thigh or shaking her fist after errors. At the end, it was Venus who pulled out the 6-2, 7-6 victory after Serena served a double fault on match point.

Venus enjoyed a subdued victory while consoling her younger sister, who was visibly upset by her loss. Venus knew how much Serena hated to lose. She knew how deeply it hurt. Venus told reporters, "I'm always the big sister. I always take care of Serena, no matter what. I always make the decisions. I'm always a role model for Serena. I'm the big sister. I always worry about her."[17] Zina Garrison, a former top-10 player who had mentored Serena over the years, understood that sibling component. She told the *New York Times*: "I know from being the youngest [sibling], no matter what I accomplish, or what I do, my big sisters felt that they could dominate me."[18] Garrison also said that Venus was on her game for this match: "Today, Venus basically showed

Venus Williams leaps into the air after defeating defending champion Lindsay Davenport to win the women's singles final at Wimbledon on July 8, 2000. Williams wins the final 6-3, 7-6 (7-3).

that she really wants this tournament. No matter who she played today, she would have won."[19]

When the match ended, the crowd watched Venus and Serena approach each other at the net, where big sister gave little sister a hug. Venus was happy to have won the match and advance to the finals, but she was unhappy that Serena was hurting. Venus whispered in Serena's ear, "Let's get out of here." [20]

Although Serena was disappointed in her performance at the tournament, she was proud of her sister, who beat Lindsay Davenport to win her first Grand Slam singles title. Another of Venus's dreams had come true, winning the title her father had said she would years ago. Venus told the Centre Court crowd after her 6-3, 7-6 win: "It's really great because I've been working so hard all my life to be here."[21] With the victory, Venus became the first African American to win Wimbledon since Althea Gibson in 1958. And Venus and Serena became the first sisters ever to each hold a Grand Slam title. The following day, Venus and Serena won the women's double title by defeating Julie Halard-Decugis and Ai Sugiyama.

CONTINUED SUCCESS

Venus and Serena both took part in the U.S. Open in September 2000. Would there be a sister-sister match in the finals? Would Serena be able to defend her U.S. Open title from the previous year? Or would Venus continue her winning streak and take home a second straight Grand Slam title?

Serena started out with her usual power in the early rounds but lost to Lindsay Davenport in the quarterfinals. She also had to withdraw from the doubles tournament with Venus because of inflammation in her left foot. There would be no sister-sister final, but Serena would be cheering her sister on to win the singles title.

Venus beat her semifinal opponent, Martina Hingis. Then she faced Lindsay Davenport (whom Venus had beaten in the Wimbledon final earlier in the year) in the finals. Venus won in straight sets and earned a second Grand Slam singles title. At this point, Venus had won 26 consecutive matches.

The sisters, both healthy and playing well, headed to Sydney, Australia, in September to take part in the 2000 Summer Olympics. Venus would take home a gold medal in women's singles after beating Elena Dementieva. And Serena, just a week before her nineteenth birthday, was happy to team up with Venus to take on the Dutch team in the doubles final. Before the match, the sisters had trained with tennis greats Billie Jean King and Zina Garrison. King told reporters, "[Venus and Serena] listen very well. They really want to improve."[22] King and Garrison worked with the women to improve their volleys and synchronize their doubles movement. The hard work paid off. Venus and Serena easily beat Miriam Oremans and Kristie Boogert of the Netherlands. Venus told the *New York Times*, "For me, [winning the gold medal in doubles] is almost bigger than singles. It's right up there because I have this victory with Serena, my sister, my family member, my best friend."[23]

Two months later, *Sports Illustrated for Women* named Venus Williams Sportswoman of the Year. Venus and Serena together received the Women's Sports Foundation Sportswomen of the Year team award for their doubles win at Wimbledon and the Olympic Games. The Williams sisters seemed unstoppable.

Making Dreams Come True

The year 2000 had been a terrific one for the Williams sisters, who looked forward to continuing success in the new year. Unfortunately, they hit a snag at the 2001 Australian Open. Suffering from food poisoning, Serena lost to Martina Hingis in the quarterfinals (even though she led 4-1 in the third set). Venus, too, had a rough quarterfinal, but she managed to pull off a three-set victory over Amanda Coetzer. Then, in the semifinal, Venus lost to Hingis. The sisters did see success in the doubles tournament, however, winning the Australian Open doubles title for the first time.

CONTROVERSY
The 2001 Tennis Masters Series at Indian Wells seemed to promise a Williams semifinal. Each sister had shown

complete control and power in her quarterfinal match. Serena easily defeated Lindsay Davenport, and Venus quickly beat Elena Dementieva. Venus (ranked third in the world) and Serena (ranked sixth) were set to play against each other in the semifinals.

The matchup, though, never happened. Just four minutes before the semifinal was to begin, Venus announced that she was withdrawing from the competition because of tendinitis in her knee. As a result, Serena—without having played a semifinal—would head to the finals against Kim Clijsters.

Fans booed the announcement, and reporters buzzed over the news. People asked if the withdrawal had been staged. The Williams sisters had heard these accusations before. Richard Williams had become known to exaggerate to make a point or liven up an event. His insistence that his daughters would become ranked No. 1 and No. 2 in the world had fueled rumors that the sisters fixed their matches. Richard became angry after hearing that Dementieva had told reporters that he would decide the winner of the semifinal between Venus and Serena. Asked about Venus's injury in a phone interview, Richard snapped, "How would I know? I'm not even there."[1]

Venus, however, was calm in the face of such insinuations. She told reporters, "It's not a true opinion. Everyone makes their own comments. That's how rumors get started. I guess the rumors are more exciting than the truth. The truth is I'm suffering from an injury, and I'm really looking to get back for the Ericsson [tournament]."[2]

As the rumors swirled, the Williams family caught the brunt of it when Serena took to the court two days later to face Kim Clijsters in the final. As Richard and Venus made their way to their seats, the crowd booed them. According to Richard, the taunts had racial overtones. Richard claimed that one man threatened to skin him alive.

The crowd also booed Serena during her match against Clijsters. Serena was hurt by the crowd's reaction and lost the first set because she let her emotions get the best of her. But she pulled herself together and pushed the crowd out of her mind. She had had no part in Venus's withdrawal; she was not going to pay the price. Serena fought back with all her strength and power to take down Clijsters. Her victory received a mixed reaction of boos and applause. When Serena accepted her trophy and the $330,000 prize check, she told the crowd, "I'd like to thank everyone who supported me, and if you didn't, I love you guys anyway."[3] Nonetheless, the Williams family vowed never to play at Indian Wells again.

At the next tournament, the Ericsson Open, Serena lost her quarterfinal match to Jennifer Capriati. Serena was suffering from an injured quadriceps muscle, which left her unable to perform at her full potential. (After leaving the tour in 1994, Capriati came back in 1996 and began to rise in the rankings; in 2001, she won her first Grand Slam title at the Australian Open.) The Ericsson crowd welcomed Venus, who quickly eliminated Miriam Oremans in her first match. She went on to beat Hingis in the semifinals and Capriati in the final. When reporters asked how she had felt over the past few weeks with all the controversy surrounding Indian Wells, Venus said, "Just hanging in there through it all. Through all the tough matches, through any ridiculous comments or questions I had to face."[4] It was Venus's third Ericsson singles title win.

In the next Grand Slam, the French Open, Barbara Schett unexpectedly knocked out Venus in the first round. After Venus lost, she and Serena withdrew from the doubles event, and Venus immediately flew home. Serena, however, continued on to make the quarterfinals. In that round, Serena, who looked sluggish and tired, fell to Capriati in a three-set match.

In July 2001, Serena again lost to Capriati in the quarterfinals, this time at Wimbledon. Throughout the match, Serena had to deal with a stomach virus that required occasional assistance from the trainer; Venus's quarterfinal match went more smoothly. After allowing Nathalie Tauziat to come back from a 5-1 deficit in the first set, Venus found her rhythm and was able to defeat Tauziat. Then, Venus overcame Lindsay Davenport in three sets in the semifinals. She went on to win her second consecutive Wimbledon championship and her third Grand Slam singles title when she defeated Justine Henin, 6-1, 3-6, 6-0.

Meanwhile, Serena faced more health problems throughout the 2001 season. She had to withdraw from the Open Gaz de France because of fatigue, the Scottsdale tournament because of the flu, and the Charleston tournament, the Italian Open, and the Madrid tournament because of knee injuries. It was clear by August that Serena had regained her form while playing at the Rogers AT&T Cup in Toronto, where she beat Capriati to take the title.

NO. 1 AND NO. 2

At the 2001 U.S. Open, Serena had to come from behind in the opening round to beat Anca Barna. She also needed three sets to defeat Davenport in the quarterfinals before handily beating Hingis in the semifinal. Venus had cruised through her matches, taking down Capriati in the semifinal with her strong backhand. Venus and Serena were to meet for the first time in a Grand Slam final.

Venus prevailed, 6-2, 6-4, taking home the title, her second U.S. Open and her fourth Grand Slam singles title. The match marked the first time a women's final was televised in prime time; the rating was 51 percent higher than the 2000 U.S. Open women's final. An estimated 22.2 million people watched all or part of the match. It was also the first Grand Slam final between siblings in 117 years,

Venus Williams, left, and her sister Serena share a laugh during the trophy ceremony following Serena's defeat at Venus's hands in the women's finals at the U.S. Open tennis tournament in New York on September 8, 2001.

since Maud and Lillian Watson played in the Wimbledon women's singles final.

At the net after the match Venus wrapped Serena in an embrace and whispered, "I love you"[5] in her ear. Later, in front of a crowd of more than 23,000, Venus said, "I always want Serena to win. It's strange. I'm the bigger sister. I'm the one who takes care of her. I make sure she has everything even if I don't. I love her. It's hard."[6] Along with her trophy, Venus accepted $850,000 in prize money.

Serena won her own title at the year-end WTA Tour Championships, where she advanced to the finals with little difficulty. There, she would have faced Davenport, who had to withdraw because of a knee injury. By default, Serena won the prestigious title.

Venus continued her winning ways, too, in early 2002. She won a tournament in Gold Coast, Australia, and made it to the quarterfinals of the Australian Open. (Serena did not play the Australian Open because of an injury.) In February, she won consecutive tournaments in Paris and Antwerp, Belgium. Late in the month, she attained the No. 1 ranking on the women's tour. Serena helped her sister keep that ranking by defeating Jennifer Capriati in the finals of the State Farm Classic in Scottsdale, Arizona. And with her win, Serena moved up from No. 9 to No. 6 in the world.

The sisters went on to play great tennis at the Nasdaq-100 Open, with both ending up in the semifinals against each other. This time, little sister Serena showed dominance and control; she won the match in less than an hour. Serena had fewer errors and was ready for Venus's second serves. Serena faced Capriati in the finals and, after a tie-breaker in the second set, won the tournament. The victory earned Serena $385,000 in prize money.

Serena lost in the 2002 German Open finals in Berlin to Justine Henin. The final was Serena's first in a clay-court tournament. Days after the German Open, Serena played in the Italian Open in Rome and advanced to the semifinals. Although Venus had to withdraw from the tournament because of an injured right wrist, she was there to watch Serena defeat Capriati in a three-set match in the semifinal. Then Serena beat Henin to claim her first tournament victory on clay. She told reporters, "A lot of people insist I'm not a clay-court player, although I am. So it makes me feel really good, especially going into Roland Garros."[7]

And Serena did feel confident as she went into the 2002 French Open at Roland Garros. In a telephone interview, Serena confessed, "I think nowadays I'm very focused. I don't believe many people can beat me, if any. I think that's the difference. I just think now if I play well, it's hard to overcome me. I think Venus has had that attitude for a long while. Now, I've been able to develop it."[8]

At the French Open, Venus defeated Monica Seles in the quarterfinals and then took out Clarisa Fernández in the semifinals. She had made it to the final. Meanwhile, Serena was able to outwit Capriati in a three-set match to ensure her own spot in the final. Although Serena had to work hard to win her match, she later told a reporter, "I never think of losing, because when you start thinking negative thoughts, negative things happen. I just always think positive, keep fighting."[9] Just like that, Richard's declaration from years before had become a reality: Regardless of who won the final, his daughters were going to be ranked No. 1 and No. 2 in the world.

The 2002 French Open title went to Serena, who beat Venus for the first time in a Slam. Serena now had two Grand Slam singles titles. At the end of the competition, Serena held the trophy—the Coupe Suzanne Lenglen— high above her head. It was the first time in tennis history that sisters held the top two rankings.

HOLDING ON

The 2002 Wimbledon was the next Slam. Would the top-two-ranked sisters see each other again in the final? In an early round, Serena had difficulties against Els Callens, but won both sets in tiebreakers. Serena later told reporters, "I was a bit nervous to move because every time I seemed to want to move, I would slip or fall or something, especially in the first set. It was like everything I did, I kept on falling."[10] Both sisters, however, made the semifinals. Venus first beat Justine Henin; then Serena defeated Amélie

ANGELA HAYNES

Venus and Serena Williams have opened the door to other African Americans who otherwise might not have seen tennis as an option, including Angela Haynes.

At the 2004 U.S. Open, history was made when four African-American women moved into the third round. They were Venus and Serena Williams, Chanda Rubin, and Angela Haynes, who was then just 20 years old.

Haynes was born in September 1984. When she was just four years old, her older brother and sister were practicing with Venus and Serena in Compton. Although Haynes was too little to join in at the time, she fell in love with tennis and played her first tournament when she was just seven.

After turning professional, Haynes defeated Rita Grande to win the Bank of the West Classic in 2003. She also won a singles title at Hilton Head, South Carolina, in 2007. Haynes reached her career-high singles ranking at No. 95 in 2005; she reached her career-high doubles ranking at No. 101 in 2006.

Mauresmo. Once again, Venus and Serena would meet in the final—their third in the last four majors. But who would take home the trophy and the title?

The match was competitive, and neither sister looked ready to back down. Serena, though, continued her winning streak with strong serves and an unrelenting approach to her game. Between sets, she studied her notes. She stayed focused and got past Venus, 7-6, 6-3, to claim her third Grand Slam title. Venus and Serena then won the Wimbledon doubles title over Virginia Ruano Pascual and Paola Suárez.

In September 2002, Venus and Serena were hoping to meet in another all-sister final in the U.S. Open. Serena easily took out Dinara Safina, who was making her Grand Slam debut, in the second round. Clad in a tennis outfit sporting a hot-pink top, Serena beat Dája Bedáňová in a quick fourth-round match. Later, Serena downed Lindsay Davenport to ensure herself a spot in the final. Venus had faced Amélie Mauresmo a few hours before Serena's match; it took three sets, but Venus came out with the win. The final was decided—it would be another Venus vs. Serena matchup.

Three straight sister-sister Grand Slams were making the news. Some people thought the matches lacked interest because neither sister played to her potential. Others thought that the matchups were bad for tennis. Venus took offense. She told reporters, "I don't see why the question could be relevant, why it would be bad for tennis. It's never been asked before."[11]

Serena again beat Venus for her third-straight Grand Slam singles title. Only six other women in history had won three consecutive majors in a calendar year. Serena, who had missed the Australian Open with an injury, called her accomplishment a Serena Slam. Venus, always gracious in a loss, was ready to return to Florida. The relentlessness

Serena Williams runs to the net after defeating her sister Venus in the women's final at the U.S. Open in New York on September 7, 2002.

of the media's questions had left her tired. She admitted to a reporter, "I just have to tune out everything; people just wear you to death, talk so much. I just want to get away from the hype."[12]

After the Open, Serena chalked up two more WTA Tour victories, winning the Toyota Princess Cup in Tokyo and the Sparkassen Cup in Leipzig, Germany. A month later, at the year-end WTA Tour Championships in Los Angeles, Serena beat Anna Smashnova in the first round. Although the match was one-sided, Serena still wowed the crowds with her fashionable ensemble of a salmon-colored dress, matching shoes, and headband.

Venus and Serena both made it to the semifinals of the tournament, but Venus, in a match against Kim Clijsters, had to retire because of a leg injury after only 13 minutes of play. Serena, on the other hand, came back from a set down to defeat Jennifer Capriati. Instead of facing Venus, Serena would take on Clijsters in the final. Clijsters held on for the victory to end Serena's 18-match winning streak.

Despite the end-of-season loss, Serena Williams had had an incredible year; she had been ranked No. 1 in the world since July 2002. The Associated Press named her Female Athlete of the Year. She had won three of the four Slam titles, 56 out of the 61 matches she had played, and eight of the 13 tournaments she entered. She had always made it at least to the quarterfinals; twice she was runner-up. Serena's tennis game was at an all-time best.

Venus had also had an incredible year and was ranked No. 2 in the world for half of it. She and Serena held on to their No. 1 and No. 2 spots, despite competing in only about half as many tournaments as most Women's Tennis Association players. While most players average 24 tournaments a year, Venus and Serena each averaged about 13. Yet they were still top tennis players.

Keeping
the Balance

Ever since they were young girls hitting hundreds of balls a day on the beat-up courts of Compton, the Williams sisters had dreamed of being tennis champions. Now they had accomplished that dream: They were dominating the game, frequently meeting in finals and snatching up titles. Venus and Serena, though, have kept in mind that life is not all about tennis. Their parents tried to instill a sense of balance in their lives. They both knew that too much tennis would not be good for them.

PRIVATE LIVES

In April 2002, 21-year-old Venus found some balance for her life when she took on a new venture: interior design. The previous year, Venus had stopped her schooling at the

Art Institute of Fort Lauderdale. She had not completed her degree, but she went on to receive a degree through the London-based Rhodec International correspondence school.

With her degree completed, Venus launched V Starr Interiors, a firm that specializes in interior design; celebrity clients have included baseball pitcher Brad Penny and sister Serena. Venus's first client came from the Stone Creek Ranch development in Delray Beach, Florida, where she designed four rooms for a model interior. Unfortunately, only a year after V Starr opened, the Florida Board of Architecture and Interior Design found out that Venus had been operating without a license and issued a cease-and-desist order; the firm temporarily closed. By the end of 2003, however, Venus had obtained the proper licenses and V Starr Interiors officially reopened.

Venus works with a team of four designers. The design team does various projects for clients, from simple accessorizing to elaborate design work that entails architects and carpenters. Venus enjoys designing custom pieces and using natural stone, silk, and lots of color.

Venus told an interviewer that her outside interests do not interfere with her tennis: "I work hard at everything I do. You know, I play tennis, but also I am a normal person, so I do my best at everything. . . . I enjoy playing, I enjoy my life. I enjoy all the blessings that I receive. I think there are so many people who would love to be in my position. So I'll take advantage of it and keep enjoying it."[1] The enjoyment that Venus has found in V Starr combines her love of design, travel, antiques, and art. Her work there helps her keep the balance she knows life requires.

Serena, too, began to seek a balance between tennis and outside interests. She bought a new apartment in Los Angeles, California, just a couple of years after she and Venus had built their home in Palm Beach Gardens,

Venus Williams poses in a room decorated by V Starr, her interior design company, on June 10, 2004. The room is inside a newly designed home in Delray Beach, Florida.

Florida. Serena still returns to the Florida house but she spends much of her time in California. When Serena is away, Venus spends her time sewing, renting movies, and tending to the family dogs—when she isn't busy with V Starr Interiors. In California, Serena is able to pursue her own love: acting. She has even appeared on television, including in an episode of ABC's *My Wife and Kids* and an episode of Showtime's *Street Time*.

Like Venus, Serena studied at the Art Institute of Fort Lauderdale. In June 2004, Serena started her own fashion line called Aneres (her name spelled backward). To run Aneres, Serena has offices in Palm Beach Gardens, Florida; Los Angeles, California; and Florence, Italy. Serena works closely with designers to make her fashion visions come to life. Models have worn Serena's clothing on the covers of high-fashion magazines like *Elle*, *Glamour*, and *Vogue*. Serena also uses her clothing line to help raise money for cancer research, the OWL Foundation (which was founded by Oracene to finance programs to help children with learning problems), and other charities.

HEALTH PROBLEMS RESURFACE

Venus and Serena both headed to the 2003 Australian Open, where they hoped to pick up where they left off in 2002. As each battled her way to the semifinals, it seemed both were destined for another good year. Venus's semifinal was against Justine Henin-Hardenne, whom she easily defeated. Venus had control over the game, and the outcome was not surprising. Serena, on the other hand, had a difficult time against her opponent, Kim Clijsters. Twice, Serena found herself close to losing the match, but she came back to fend off the match points. In the third set, Serena was down 1-5 but came back to win.

It was the first time either sister had made it to an Australian Open final. For the fourth time in a row, a Grand

During one of her forays into acting, Serena Williams appears with Bernie Mac on a 2006 episode of his hit sitcom *The Bernie Mac Show*.

Slam final featured sister against sister. And for the fourth time in a row, Serena beat Venus, 7-6, 3-6, 6-4, resulting in Serena becoming one of five women ever to have held all four Slam titles at one time. (The last person to do so was Steffi Graf in 1994.) Serena also took home the title in the women's doubles, along with Venus.

Venus and Serena had kept their father's prediction going—they remained No. 1 and No. 2 in the world of tennis. Getting to the top had to do with cultivating the right combination of natural ability and dedicated practice. The sisters have believed they could do it from the time they were young. Their parents supported their dream and helped them set goals to achieve it. But how long could their dominance continue?

Serena was not about to lose her top ranking. In February, she took home the title at the Open Gaz de France by defeating Amélie Mauresmo. Later in the month, though, she had to withdraw from the State Farm Classic in Scottsdale, Arizona, just an hour before competition, because of tendinitis in her left knee. Rebounding from that injury, Serena took home the Nasdaq-100 Open title in March when she defeated Jennifer Capriati. In April, Serena finally suffered a loss when Henin-Hardenne took the Family Circle Cup title. Two months later, Serena was knocked out of the Italian Open, losing to Mauresmo in the semifinals.

DID YOU KNOW?

In 2005, Venus and Serena appeared on their own reality television program; they also served as executive producers on the show. They wanted to portray women working (at tennis and in design), being successful, and leading happy, fulfilled lives. Because the sisters see themselves as role models, they thought a reality program that showed young people how to be competitive and fun would be beneficial.

The show, *Venus and Serena: For Real,* ran for five episodes from July 20 to August 17 on the ABC Family network. The show depicted the sisters' hectic schedules and gave viewers a look at life on the tennis courts. During one episode, Serena was in the stands with a boyfriend, while Venus played a match. Serena thought that the cameras were only taping Venus's game. She was surprised when she later saw footage of her and her boyfriend breaking up, but she let the footage air anyway, because she thought the segment turned out fine.

At the 2003 French Open, Venus was defeated in the fourth round by Vera Zvonareva in the semifinals to Henin-Hardenne. Serena lost the first set, won the second, and was winning the third. Then, when Serena was about to serve, she saw Henin-Hardenne put up her hand to signal that she was not ready. So instead of serving, Serena swatted the ball into the net, waiting to hear the umpire call a let. The umpire, however, did not see Henin-Hardenne signal that she was not ready, and Henin-Hardenne did not admit that she had done so. No let was called, and the serve was considered a fault. The match became more difficult for Serena, as the crowd greatly favored the French-speaking Henin-Hardenne. The crowd began to boo Serena relentlessly from the stands. They even started to cheer when Serena made a mistake. She was unable to hold her lead in the third set and lost. By the end of the match, Serena was crying

In the spring of 2003, both Venus and Serena struggled with injuries. Venus pulled muscles in her stomach, which caused her to miss matches. When she did play in a tournament, she had her abs tightly wrapped to help ease the pain.

At the 2003 Wimbledon tournament, Serena again faced Henin-Hardenne in the semifinals. This time no crowd was booing, and there were no unseen hand signals. Serena easily won the match. Later, Venus won her own semifinal against Kim Clijsters, despite obvious pain from her strained stomach muscle. In the final against Serena, Venus had to have her stomach rewrapped in the third set. Serena won soon after to capture her sixth Grand Slam singles title.

During Serena's Wimbledon doubles competition, she reinjured her left knee. After meeting with her physician, Dr. Rodney Gabriel, Serena learned that she required knee surgery, after which she would need months of recuperation and rehabilitation before she could play tennis again.

Serena was at the top of her game, ranked No. 1; she hated to step out of competition. Still, she knew the surgery was necessary. As a result, she was unable to play in a number of tournaments, including the Bank of the West Classic, the Acura Classic, the Canadian Open, and the U.S. Open. Because of her absence from the game, Serena lost her No. 1 ranking; Clijsters was now on top.

The abdominal pain that Venus felt during Wimbledon left her off the court as well. While Venus and Serena were recovering, they used the time to read, work on their design projects, and keep their bodies in shape through rehabilitation exercises. Serena also did some acting and fashion shows. They used the time to focus on themselves and their other interests. When her contract with Puma expired, Serena signed a multimillion-dollar deal with Nike to appear in its "What If?" commercials. Serena would be appearing as a beach volleyball player. Despite their many activities, both sisters were looking forward to getting back on the tennis court.

During this time away from tennis, the sisters suffered a severe blow. Tragedy struck in September 2003, when Venus and Serena learned of the death of their half-sister Yetunde Price. Price was shot while sitting in a car during a confrontation with a group of people on a street in Compton. Price, a 31-year-old single mother, had three children. Yetunde's death shocked the entire Williams family. She had been a voice of encouragement to the family, one who had pointed out the positives. They could only strive to continue that outlook now and stand together as they dealt with this loss.

ORACENE PRICE

Venus and Serena's mother has always been a strong force in their lives. In the preface of the book *Serving from the Hip*, Oracene wrote that, when the girls were young, she would tell them, "If you work hard now, it will be easy later."[2] But she also wanted them to know that she and Richard would never force them to play tennis if they did not want to. She said to them, "If anytime you feel like you want to quit [tennis], you can. You don't have to do this to be successful. Whatever you do, I'm proud of you."[3]

In 2002, Richard and Oracene separated and then divorced, citing irreconcilable differences. (Oracene then took her maiden name, Price.) Although no longer married, Richard and Oracene continue to support Venus and Serena as a united front. Both parents still give coaching advice when asked. Above all, they continue to support and love their children. Oracene and her daughter Isha are frequently seen in the family box at matches, cheering on Venus and/or Serena. And Richard either attends the matches or watches on television.

Oracene, who believes in a strong family base, is happy to see her daughters leading fulfilled lives. Oracene and Richard did not allow the sisters to date until they turned 18. Since then, Oracene has urged all of her daughters to remain single. In an interview with *Ebony* magazine, Oracene said that she told her girls, "Don't get married. Don't rush yourself. Live life. Freedom is a blessing."[4]

So far, Venus and Serena have done just that. Serena enjoys going out with friends and going to clubs and parties, and she has yet to settle into marriage. Over the years, she has dated football players LaVar Arrington and Keyshawn Johnson, actor Jackie Long, and, most recently, the rapper Common. She is attracted to men who are athletically fit, spiritual, polite, and able to make her laugh. Venus enjoys spending time with her longtime boyfriend, PGA Tour golfer Hank Kuehne.

Because they have busy schedules, the sisters make time to spend with their mother. Serena describes Oracene as fun and easygoing. All three women love to laugh and enjoy one another's sense of humor. Oracene is proud of her well-rounded daughters. She recognizes and appreciates their self-confidence, their levelheadedness, and their kindness.

FINDING A PLACE BACK ON THE COURT

Venus returned to competition first, with her abs healed and her body conditioned. She even won an exhibition tournament in Hong Kong. But shortly afterward, in a match in Tokyo, she injured her knee. At the 2004 Australian Open (a competition Serena withdrew from beforehand), Venus twisted her ankle, reinjured her knee, and lost in the third round. It seemed that the injuries would never end. At this point, Venus had fallen in rank to No. 11 and Serena had fallen to No. 3. Once again, the sisters took time away from the game to recover. When they did enter a tournament, they often found themselves in an unusual position—on the losing end of a match.

Serena's first competition after her knee surgery was the 2004 Nasdaq-100 Open, which was held in Key Biscayne, Florida. Venus played in this tournament as well. Venus

IN HER OWN WORDS

The Williams sisters treasure their family relationships. As Serena said in *Serving from the Hip*:

> Long before fans and reporters knew [Venus and me], our parents taught us that our relationship is much more important than being successful in tennis or getting ahead in the world. Our friendship with each other and our other sisters is one of the most important and fun aspects of our lives.

made it to the quarterfinals and was even ahead in her match, but her long time away from the game had left her more out of shape than she realized. Unable to hang onto her lead, she was knocked out of the tournament by Elena Dementieva.

Serena, who had now dropped to sixth in the world, felt nervous in her first match at the Nasdaq-100 but easily defeated Marta Marrero. Serena came onto the court wearing a white dress with a billowy skirt covered by a silver corset designed by Nike, her new sponsor. In her hair, she wore a scarf with "Serena" spelled out in rhinestones. With each match Serena won, she felt more at ease and comfortable being back on the court. She advanced to the finals and took the title in a commanding victory over Dementieva.

In April, however, Serena's knee trouble led her to lose to Nadia Petrova in the quarterfinals of the Bausch & Lomb Championships. At the 2004 Italian Open, Jennifer Capriati knocked Serena out of the finals.

In May, the Williams sisters were at the French Open. In the first round, Venus defeated Tamarine Tanasugarn, and Serena beat Iveta Benešová. Serena drew attention with her fuchsia outfit that left her midriff bare, showing off her diamond-pierced bellybutton. She was also wearing a red flower in her hair. Serena next faced Maria Kirilenko, who nearly won, but Serena fought back. Venus also won her second-round match against Jelena Kostanić. The sisters continued to cruise into the quarterfinals, but there they stumbled. Capriati beat Serena, and Anastasia Myskina, the eventual champion, defeated Venus.

At the 2004 Wimbledon, Venus fell in the second round. Serena, though, showed signs of her pre-surgery self when she defeated Capriati in just 45 minutes in the quarterfinals. She then beat Amélie Mauresmo in a much closer three-set match to ensure herself a spot in the finals. There she faced a rising star, 17-year-old Maria Sharapova.

In a bit of a shocker, Sharapova won a convincing victory over Serena, 6-1, 6-4.

In August 2004, Serena withdrew from the Olympics just hours before Venus and the American tennis team boarded the airplane for Athens, Greece. Unfortunately, Serena's knee was again causing her problems. As a result, Venus played doubles with Chanda Rubin. Venus did not earn a medal in either the doubles or the women's singles, as she had in 2000.

In the 2004 U.S. Open, Serena beat Sandra Kleinová on opening night. In the next round, she took out Lindsay Lee-Waters. Much of the talk about the match revolved around Serena's outfit, which included a tight-fitting black jacket over a studded black tank top that stopped short to reveal her diamond belly ring. The ensemble also featured skintight black short shorts and knee-high black tennis boots, or gaiters.

In the quarterfinals, Jennifer Capriati took away any hopes of Serena winning the U.S. Open title with a three-set, come-from-behind victory. Several questionable calls went against Serena. Two balls that Serena hit appeared to land on the baseline, but both times the balls were called out. At another point, it looked as though Capriati double-faulted, which would have given Serena a break point. The fault, however, was not called. Serena argued with the chair umpire, who incorrectly overruled the line judge. Later, the United States Tennis Association (USTA) apologized to Serena for the unfair calls. They also commended Serena for her graciousness in dealing with the press. In interviews Serena had made a point of saying that she did not blame her loss on the calls but that she had simply played poorly. Venus, too, had a disappointing Grand Slam, falling in the fourth round to Lindsay Davenport.

In November 2004, Serena beat Mauresmo in a three-set match during the semifinals of the WTA Tour

Championships in Los Angeles. Again in the finals, she faced Maria Sharapova, who had beaten Serena at Wimbledon. Once again, Sharapova pulled out a win. During the second set, Serena pulled an abdominal muscle and needed icing from her trainer at changeovers.

At the end of 2004, Venus and Serena debuted the McDonald's Williams Sisters Tour, which they hoped to turn into an annual charity event. The sisters took part in exhibition matches against each other in Chicago, Illinois; Detroit, Michigan; and Atlanta, Georgia. The money they raised from ticket sales was given to Ronald McDonald House Charities as well as to local charities in each city where they played.

HEALTH ISSUES STRIKE AGAIN

The Williams sisters had mixed results in the 2005 Australian Open. Alicia Molik defeated Venus in the fourth round. Serena had a better time, finding herself in the semifinals after beating Mauresmo in the quarterfinals. She went on to beat Sharapova in a three-set match. In the finals, Serena defeated Lindsay Davenport to win her seventh Grand Slam singles title.

IN HER OWN WORDS

One attribute the Williams sisters share is perseverance. As Venus said in *Serving from the Hip*:

> I was willing to work toward my dream every day, even when I didn't feel like it. Champions don't let anything stand in their way. To make it to the top, you have to stick to your goal no matter what.

In March, at the Nasdaq-100 Open in Key Biscayne, Florida, Venus finally took a win over her younger sister. Her victory in the quarterfinals was Venus's first over Serena after six straight losses. In an interview following the match, Venus said, "I feel I have a little bit more in my game right now. I'm not sure why. I guess I'm training harder now."[5] Venus, however, lost her chance to win the tournament when she fell to Sharapova in the semifinals.

Suffering from an ankle injury, Serena did not play in the French Open, and Venus lost there in the third round. In June, both sisters were ready for Wimbledon. This time, Serena lost in an upset to Jill Craybas in the third round. Venus avenged her sister's loss by beating Craybas in the next round. In fact, Venus was in top form, cruising to the finals without losing a set in any of her matches.

When she faced Lindsay Davenport in the finals, Venus had a third Wimbledon singles title on the line. Venus rose to the challenge and displayed sheer determination and phenomenal athleticism to become the first woman to win at Wimbledon after saving a match point since Helen Wills Moody did it in 1935. At two hours and 45 minutes, the match—which Venus won 4-6, 7-6, 9-7—was the longest women's final in Wimbledon history. Venus jumped for joy upon winning and sought out her family in the stands to enjoy the moment with them. She told reporters, "I was the 14th seed. I wasn't supposed to win. I guess whoever put a bet on me really came in good on that at the beginning of the tournament. But I always bet on myself."[6] Venus, who now had five Grand Slam titles, had won her first Slam since 2001.

At the U.S. Open in September 2005, Venus and Serena faced off against each other in the fourth round. Although Venus won, she lost to Kim Clijsters in the quarterfinal.

The new year began with some letdowns. At the Australian Open in Melbourne in January 2006, Venus lost in the opening round after making numerous errors against Tszvetana Pironkova. Serena made it through two rounds but then lost to Daniela Hantuchová. In April, both Venus and Serena withdrew from the Family Circle Cup in Charleston, South Carolina, because of injuries. Venus was nursing a right elbow sprain, and Serena had a left knee injury.

By May, however, Venus was feeling better and was able to enter the J&S Cup in Warsaw, Poland. In the first round, Venus easily beat Urszula Radwańska. In the second round, Venus fought back after being down a set and suffering leg cramps to win over Martina Hingis. Venus lost in the third round to Svetlana Kuznetsova.

A week later, Venus headed to Rome, Italy, for the Internazionali BNL d'Italia, a tournament that occurs just before the French Open. Venus dominated in the early rounds, but she struggled against Jelena Janković in the quarterfinals. The heat tested the players' endurance, but after three sets, Venus came out the winner. In the semifinals, Venus faced Hingis, and although Venus won the first set, she lost the next two.

Still, Venus felt happy to be healthy and playing tennis once again. She was ready for the French Open. Serena, however, withdrew from the tournament because of her bad knee. Venus held on to win her first match, despite some solid tennis from her opponent, Sybille Bammer. In the next round, Venus had a slow start but came back strong to beat Emma Laine. In the third round, Venus defeated Karolina Šprem. Venus felt she had improved from her second-round match; she thought her serve and movement were better against Šprem than they had been against Laine. Venus won her fourth match, too, over Patty Schnyder, despite losing the first set. In the quarterfinals, however, Venus won the first set, but lost the next two, and the match, to Nicole Vaidišová. Her Grand Slam quest was over.

Venus did not back down. She looked ahead to the next Slam—Wimbledon. Once again, she would be traveling alone; Serena had withdrawn because of her knee. Venus came out strong against Bethanie Mattek; in the second round, she faced Lisa Raymond, who forced Venus to step up her game. But she responded and won the match. In the third round, Venus was up against Jelena Janković, who played well. Despite a competitive first set and a second-set win, Venus lost the match. She would not be defending her title.

Following her disappointing Wimbledon, Venus welcomed taking part in the ESPY (Excellence in Sports Performance Yearly) Awards in Los Angeles, California. Bicycling champion Lance Armstrong hosted the event, which was held at the Kodak Theatre in Hollywood. Venus was named Best Female Tennis Player, her fourth ESPY of her career, beating Kim Clijsters, Justine Henin-Hardenne, and Amélie Mauresmo for the title.

A New Outlook

In September 2006, Venus Williams missed the U.S. Open because of an injury to her left wrist. Serena Williams returned to competitive play in the tournament but lost to Amélie Mauresmo in the fourth round. Later that month, having not competed since Wimbledon, Venus returned for the Fortis Championships, even though her wrist injury had not fully healed. When Venus faced Agnieszka Radwańska in the second round, her wrist was giving her such problems that she could not hit her two-handed backhand. Instead, she had to rely on her backhand slice. Venus lost the match.

Many fans and commentators began to wonder: What had happened to Venus and Serena Williams? They were rarely playing tennis; and when they were, they were often losing. Could they regain their dominance?

FINDING ANSWERS

Before the 2006 U.S. Open, Serena had taken a six-month break from tennis, playing little since the Australian Open. She was dealing with a number of issues—the death of her sister Yetunde, depression, and weight gain. Serena spent her time sleeping in on a daily basis for the first time in her life, watching HGTV, lying by the pool or at the beach, and learning to deal better with her emotions. Serena's mother said of her time away from tennis that it "refreshed her mind, body, and soul."[1] Oracene told *People*, "It was a spiritual awakening. She was defining who she is and being happy with it."[2]

In addition, Serena traveled to Africa for the first time, visiting Senegal in November 2006. Standing on Gorée Island, where slaves had been shipped to the Americas and the Caribbean, was an eye-opener. She said, "That just changed me. It gave me strength and courage, and it let me know that I can endure anything."[3] Then Serena went to villages in Ghana, where she helped in the efforts to protect children from malaria. Her African journey left her wanting to help more. She told *People*, "The kids were so gorgeous, it broke my heart. Now I'm just trying to get other people to realize what's going on there."[4]

Meanwhile, Venus volunteered to help promote gender equality in a partnership between UNESCO (United Nations Educational, Scientific, and Cultural Organization) and the Sony Ericsson WTA Tour. As a global promoter, she worked to raise awareness of gender-equality issues. Venus, who believes that as a role model she must help women become successful, said, "Through this partnership with UNESCO, our goal is to let women and girls throughout the world know that there are no glass ceilings, and to do our part to support programs that provide real opportunities for women to succeed in whatever they set their minds to."[5]

Venus has been at the forefront of efforts to get equal prize money. As late as 2005, both Wimbledon and the French Open paid women players less than their male counterparts. That year, Venus met with officials from both tournaments to argue for equal pay. In 2006, just before Wimbledon, she wrote an essay for a London newspaper putting forth the case for equal pay. The British prime minister and several members of Parliament endorsed Venus's arguments. Finally, in February 2007, Wimbledon announced that it would award equal prize money in all rounds to men and women. The French Open followed suit the next day.

In 2007, Venus launched a clothing line called EleVen, which would be sold at Steve & Barry's, a discount clothing chain. The collection features 120 products, including tennis shoes, sportswear, T-shirts, jackets, and jewelry. Every piece in the collection would be available at retailers for less than $20, even tennis shoes.

BACK TO THE COURTS

Serena came to the 2007 Australian Open in January ranked only eighty-first in the world. Still, she felt ready to get back into tennis. She was not in ideal shape; she had not been working out as regularly as she felt she should have. Still, she concentrated on staying focused and keeping her mind on the game. Serena defeated Mara Santangelo, Anne Kremer, Nadia Petrova, Jelena Janković, and Shahar Peer to advance to the semifinals. There, she continued her astounding run by beating Nicole Vaidišová. In the finals, she faced Maria Sharapova, the top seed in the tournament. Anyone expecting a tough battle was disappointed as Serena crushed Sharapova, 6-1, 6-2. She had won her eighth Grand Slam singles title and third Australian Open title. On the podium, she told the crowd that she was dedicating her win to her deceased sister, Yetunde.

Meanwhile, Venus was working to return to the court. She spent time hitting balls and getting back in shape. By mid-February, Venus had recovered from her wrist injury. She took part in the Regions Morgan Keegan Championships & the Cellular South Cup in Memphis, Tennessee. After her four-month leave, her rank had dipped to No. 54. Venus, though, showed she was healthy when she defeated Akiko Morigami in a three-set match. She looked even better in her second match, which she won against Caroline Wozniacki. In the quarterfinals, Venus overpowered Laura Granville in competitive sets. In the semifinals, Venus kept the pressure on Ioana Raluca Olaru and took the match. She then captured the title by dominating the final against Shahar Peer.

Venus and Serena both entered the 2007 Sony Ericsson Open in Key Biscayne, Florida, in March. In early rounds, Venus beat Yuliana Fedak and Maria Kirilenko before falling to Sharapova in the third round. Serena beat Sharapova in the next round and continued through to the finals. Facing Justine Henin in the final, Serena lost the first set, 6-0, but came back strong to win the title.

At the French Open in May, Serena managed to win her second- and third-round matches even though she said she had trouble finding her rhythm. She felt more on her game when she beat Dinara Safina in the fourth round. Serena again played poorly in the quarterfinals, losing in two sets to Henin. Serena later described the match as one of the worst she had ever played. Venus, too, had a disappointing French Open, going out in the third round to Jelena Janković.

Both sisters hoped to do better at Wimbledon. Serena's fourth-round match against Daniela Hantuchová proved memorable. Serena won the first set. In the second set, with the score tied 5-5, Serena suddenly grabbed her calf and hit at it with her racket. When Serena tried to take a step, she fell to the ground. A trainer applied ice to her calf and massaged it. During 10 minutes of treatment, Serena's screams punctuated Centre Court. Despite her injury, Serena managed to stay even in the set. With Serena trailing 4-2 in the tiebreaker, rain started to pelt down and the match was delayed. Two hours later, the match resumed, and even though Hantuchová won the tiebreaker, Serena was able to take the third set and the match. She then lost to Henin in the quarterfinals.

Venus, on the other hand, marched through the rounds by easily defeating Sharapova in the fourth round, Svetlana Kuznetsova in the quarterfinals, and Ana Ivanović in the semifinals. In the final, Venus continued her command of the grass court, beating Marion Bartoli, 6-4, 6-1. She had her fourth Wimbledon title and her sixth Grand Slam singles title. As the twenty-third seed, Venus was the lowest seed ever to win Wimbledon. She also was the first woman at Wimbledon to win the same prize money as the men's champion—$1.4 million.

The 2007 U.S. Open began with a special tribute to Althea Gibson, the woman who showed the world that tennis was not just a sport for white people. About the tribute, Serena said, "If it weren't for Althea, I'm not sure we would even be out here."[6]

Then the games began. Venus and Serena sailed through their early matches. In the fourth round against Bartoli, Serena looked extremely comfortable on the court and played with confident ball striking and easy movements. Serena, however, did not get past the next round, falling to Justine Henin. Venus beat Jelena Janković to earn her spot in the semifinals, where she faced Henin, who pulled out the win. The 2007 U.S. Open had come to an end for the Williams sisters.

In 2008, Serena had an Australian Open title to defend. Could she do it? She was coming off a strong 2007 and appeared capable of keeping the title. The Australian Open, however, had changed. In the past, it had been played on a green, cushioned hard court; now athletes would play on a blue hard court. The new court provided a lower-bouncing surface that provided safer and less variable playing conditions in the heat. Both sisters easily made it to the quarterfinals; neither had dropped a set in their first four matches. In the quarterfinals, though, they both lost to a pair of Serbian players—Serena to Jelena Janković, and Venus to Ana Ivanović. Serena was extremely disappointed at losing her chance to defend her Australian Open title.

Serena once again worked hard to prepare for future tournaments. Every day she trained on the court but also worked out off the court. She lifted weights in the gym, took Pilates, and practiced yoga. Serena has said in interviews, however, that she does not enjoy going to the gym. She does it because it is her job, but working out is not her idea of a fun time.

May brought with it the French Open; Serena had last won a title there in 2002. Ready and focused, Serena opened the tournament against Ashley Harkleroad and quickly took command of the match. Next, Serena faced Mathilde Johansson. Serena easily won the first set but had to work harder in the second set before closing out the victory. In the third round, however, Serena lost to Katarina Srebotnik. Venus, too, went down in the same round, falling to Flavia Pennetta.

VENUS AND SERENA: DOMINANT ONCE AGAIN

Following the French Open, Venus and Serena had to prepare for Wimbledon in June. The weather was sunny early on, making it a different experience from the previous year's Wimbledon. Serena won the first three rounds against Kaia Kanepi, Urszula Radwańska, and Amélie Mauresmo. After her third-round match, Serena told an interviewer that she liked to play Mauresmo because they had such different styles of tennis.

Venus and Serena both made the quarterfinals. Serena easily took out teenage player Agnieszka Radwańska and felt she had served well and placed her shots. In the quarterfinals, Venus defeated Tamarine Tanasugarn. In the semifinals, Venus beat Elena Dementieva. Two rain delays held up Serena's semifinal against Zheng Jie, but Serena played strong and won. For the seventh time in their careers, Venus and Serena would meet in a Slam final.

The 2008 Wimbledon final on Centre Court was intense. Beforehand, Serena joked in an interview that she would eat all the Wheaties for breakfast so Venus would not have a chance in the match. The two sisters arrived on court together, each wearing all white and each carrying a bouquet of flowers. The crowd was hushed and waiting with anticipation for what they hoped would be a competitive

DID YOU KNOW?

While in Beijing, China, for the 2008 Olympic Games, Venus and Serena made sure to collect athlete pins that competitors receive from their confederations. Venus told an interviewer at the Games:

> I'm a huge pin collector. I still have my case. I don't show people my medals; I show them my pins. If they will ask to see the medals, I will show them, but as a rule, I will always show my pins.*

*NBC Sports. http://www.nbcolympics.com/athletes/athlete=1049/bio/.

match. Margaret Thatcher, the former prime minister of Great Britain, and Billie Jean King were two of the many celebrities in the stands. Also watching were Oracene and Isha. Richard had flown home the day before; he thought the match between his two daughters was going to be too difficult to watch.

In the first set, few errors were made on either side. Serena looked strong at the start of the first set; then Venus picked up her serve. Serena had a good sense of where her sister was going to serve and kept Venus working. The match came down to serves; it was Serena who struggled on second serves, which ultimately cost her the match, 7-5, 6-4. Venus had won her fifth career Wimbledon title and her seventh Grand Slam singles title.

When she got her championship point, the celebration was muted. Normally, Venus—especially in such a close match—would have jumped up and down, but knowing that Serena was upset over the loss, Venus simply smiled to the crowd with an uplifted arm. There was no victory dance. In her remarks to the crowd, Venus said, "I can't believe it's five, but when you're in the final against Serena Williams, five seems so far away from that first point. She played so awesome. It was really a task to beat her."[7]

Later that day, the sisters faced off against Lisa Raymond and Samantha Stosur for the doubles title. Venus and Serena won the match. Although the singles loss was a blow for Serena, the doubles win gave her reason to smile. The sisters now had won three doubles titles at Wimbledon (the first in 2000 and the second in 2002); this victory was their seventh doubles title at a Grand Slam.

Venus and Serena were excited to go to the Olympic Games in Beijing, China, in the summer of 2008. They were eager to try for a gold medal in singles and in doubles. In singles, Venus and Serena were knocked out of medal contention in the quarterfinals. Serena lost to the eventual

Serena and Venus Williams celebrate after beating Anabel Medina Garrigues and Virginia Ruano Pascual of Spain in their gold medal doubles match at the 2008 Summer Olympics.

gold medalist, Russia's Elena Dementieva, while China's Na Li defeated Venus. In doubles, however, Venus and Serena prevailed over Spain's Anabel Medina Garrigues and Virginia Ruano Pascual. They dominated both sets, 6-2, 6-0, and took home the gold.

A week after the Olympic Games, Venus and Serena were participating in the U.S. Open. On a steamy August day, in the fourth round, Venus beat Agnieszka Radwańska, while Serena beat Séverine Brémond later on the same court. They had each secured a spot against the other in the quarterfinals.

Many people thought that the sisters' quarterfinal was the best match ever between them—and many also believed it should have been the final. They both showed top skill and determination, hitting balls hard and deep. The match stayed close, and each woman put up a strong performance. Although Venus had a lead in each of the sets, Serena was able to save all 10 set points to eventually win, 7-6, 7-6. Serena was on her way to the U.S. Open semifinals.

Serena faced Dinara Safina in the semifinals, where—unlike her match against Venus—she dominated the court for an easy win. She would be heading to the finals and playing to regain the Grand Slam title that she had first won in 1999. In front of a crowd of 20,000 people, Serena beat Jelena Janković to regain her top spot. The victory came when Serena hit a game-winning backhand cross-court shot. Serena had won her ninth Grand Slam singles title and her third at the U.S. Open.

In November, Venus and Serena traveled to the season-ending Sony Ericsson Championships in Doha, Qatar, where the top eight players in the world compete against one another. With a victory over Serena, Venus qualified for the semifinals. In that round, Venus defeated Jelena Janković and then took out Vera Zvonareva in the finals. Venus, who went into the event ranked No. 8, moved up to No. 6 with the victory. (Serena went into the event ranked No. 3 and came out ranked No. 2, behind Janković.) Venus took home $1.34 million in prize money for her win. Venus

(continues on page 100)

BILLIE JEAN KING

When she was five years old, Billie Jean King told her mother she was going to do something great with her life, and she did just that.

Born on November 22, 1943, she bought her first tennis racket when she was 11 and learned to play on the public

Tennis legend Billie Jean King watches her return to Bobby Riggs in the "Battle of the Sexes" match held at the Houston Astrodome on September 20, 1973. Billie Jean King accepted Riggs's challenge and beat him in a 6-4, 6-3, 6-3 wipeout that was a bold statement for a whole generation of women.

courts near her home in Long Beach, California. She played junior tennis before turning professional. Like the Williams sisters, King pushed the limits with her tennis attire. In 1955, she was barred from posing for a group photo with the other junior tennis players of the Los Angeles Tennis Club. The reason was she was wearing tennis shorts, not a tennis skirt.

King won a record 20 Wimbledon titles from 1961 to 1979 (six singles, 10 doubles, and four mixed doubles). In 1971, she became the first female athlete in any sport to win $100,000. Two years later, she began to lobby for and obtain equal prize money for women. Her campaign brought about a famous match called the "Battle of the Sexes," in which Bobby Riggs played King before a worldwide television audience. Riggs had claimed women's tennis was inferior to men's. King won the match in three sets. In 1974, King became the first president of the Women's Tennis Association, and she helped to organize the first women's tour, the Virginia Slims Tour, in the 1970s.

When Venus accepted her champion's check of $1.4 million at the 2007 Wimbledon, she told the BBC, "No one loves tennis more than Billie Jean King." * And then in an address to King, Venus added, "I love you. I wouldn't be here if it weren't for you." **

---

*George Vecsey, "Across the Net, but Still on the Same Side." *New York Times*, September 3, 2008.
**Ibid.

(continued from page 97)

now had three titles in 2008: Wimbledon, Zurich, and the Sony Ericsson Championships.

About her 2008 season, which included more than 40 victories, Serena told reporters: "That was my goal, to be more consistent, to play more tournaments. I love playing tennis and love the competition and love being out there. My goal at the beginning of the year was just to be happy every time I go out there and just play, and that was what I pretty much did this whole year."[8] Both Venus and Serena could look back on their seasons with pride: Each had improved her ranking and each had ended with a huge win. And they weren't done with tennis yet.

GIVING BACK

In November and December 2005 and 2006, Venus and Serena held their second and third annual McDonald's Williams Sisters Tour to benefit the Ronald McDonald House Charities. In 2005, the sisters took part in exhibition matches against each other in Seattle, Washington; Cleveland, Ohio; and Washington, D.C. The following year, they held exhibition matches in Denver, Colorado; New Orleans, Louisiana; and Charlotte, North Carolina. While in New Orleans, Venus and Serena also visited children at the Ronald McDonald House and attended a pep rally at Clark High School downtown. Part of the money they raised also went to help people affected by Hurricane Katrina in 2005.

In August 2008, Serena founded the Serena Williams Foundation to help young people who cannot afford to go to college. In an interview, she said, "At the end of my career, I'd love to just dedicate myself to working in philanthropy. I love giving and helping people. I think it's so awesome to be in a position to help people."[9] In November, Serena traveled to Kenya, Africa, to open a school as part of her charity work. The school, named the Serena Williams Secondary School, included a computer lab donated by Hewlett-Packard.

Serena also found time in November to participate in Pam Shriver's twenty-third annual Charity Tennis Classic along with other tennis greats. Serena faced off against Elena Dementieva, who won both matches. The crowd enjoyed the women's performances, including Serena's pretend dizzy spell after a ball hit her in the head. Before the match, kids could listen to a reading from Serena and Venus Williams's book, *Venus and Serena: Serving from the Hip: 10 Rules for Living, Loving, and Winning*.

Looking Forward

What's to come for these two women who have already accomplished so much in their short lives? This sister duo has dominated women's tennis for years. As of the end of 2008, Venus had won 16 Grand Slam titles (7 singles, 7 doubles, and 2 mixed). Serena had won 18 Grand Slam titles (9 singles, 7 doubles, and 2 mixed). And while many of their early rivals have retired from the sport—like Kim Clijsters, Justine Henin, and Martina Hingis—neither Venus nor Serena has plans to put down her racket anytime soon. For Venus and Serena, more tennis is still to come. Although they enjoy their other interests, they feel they have more Slams to win and more trophies to collect—not to mention gold medals at the 2012 Olympics in London.

The sisters, particularly Serena, continued their winning ways at the first Grand Slam tournament of the 2009 season, the Australian Open. Serena got through the first three rounds with relative ease, winning each match in straight sets. In the fourth round, she lost the first set to Victoria Azarenka. Serena began to come back in the second set when Azarenka, suffering from an illness, retired from the match. In the quarterfinals, Serena needed three sets to beat Svetlana Kuznetsova, but Serena seemed to save her best tennis for the end of the tournament. She defeated Elena Dementieva, 6-3, 6-4, in the semifinals and rolled over Dinara Safina, 6-0, 6-3, to capture her tenth Grand Slam championship. She had won consecutive Grand Slam titles for the first time in six years. With the victory, Serena again claimed the No. 1 ranking in the world.

Venus's singles run at the Australian Open ended early, as she lost in the second round. But she and her sister combined to win the doubles tournament, giving them their eighth Grand Slam women's doubles title. And Serena earned another distinction with her accomplishments at the Australian Open. With her wins, she surpassed golfer Annika Sorenstam as the women's all-time leader in prize money. Over her career, Serena has won $23.5 million.

Off the courts, the sisters continue to enrich their lives through their charity work, family, and personal interests. In 2009, Grand Central Publishing will release Serena's memoir, which is said to have a strong motivational slant. Each will continue her fashion line—EleVen for Venus and Aneres for Serena. Venus will continue to build her design business, V Starr Interiors, and Serena will continue to pursue acting opportunities.

Venus and Serena have well-grounded values. Their ability to turn dreams into reality helps them lead happy, fulfilled lives. They keep in mind that life is much more

Serena and Venus Williams photographed at the 2003 Laureus World Sports Awards held in Monte Carlo.

than tennis, and they try to approach everything they do with an open mind, a desire to increase their knowledge, and a good sense of humor. Venus and Serena Williams are best friends, elite athletes, and positive role models. They have shown the world that two African Americans from a low-income background can do more than make a name for themselves in the predominantly white, upper-class sport of tennis—they can raise the level of the game. Because of Venus and Serena Williams, the game of tennis will never be the same—it will be forever better.

CHRONOLOGY

1980   Venus Ebone Starr Williams is born on June 17 in Lynwood, California.

1981   Serena Williams is born on September 26 in Saginaw, Michigan.

1991   Venus and Serena begin to train with Rick Macci at the Rick Macci International Tennis Academy.

1994   Venus plays her first professional tennis match in October at the Bank of the West Classic. She wins her first match but loses her second.

1995   Serena plays her first professional match in October at the Bell Challenge. She loses her first-round match.

1997   As an unseeded player, Venus makes it all the way to the finals of the U.S. Open.

1998   Venus and Serena graduate from the Driftwood Academy.

1999   Serena wins her first Grand Slam singles title at the U.S. Open against Martina Hingis.

2000   Venus wins her first Grand Slam singles title at Wimbledon against Lindsay Davenport; Venus wins her second Grand Slam singles title at the U.S. Open, also against Davenport; Venus wins a gold medal in singles and she and Serena win a gold medal in doubles at the Summer Olympics.

2001   Venus wins her third Grand Slam singles title at Wimbledon against Justine Henin;

Venus wins her fourth Grand Slam singles title at the U.S. Open against Serena Williams.

2002   Serena wins her second Grand Slam singles title at the French Open against Venus Williams; Venus is ranked No. 1 and Serena is ranked No. 2; Serena wins her third Grand Slam singles title at Wimbledon against Venus Williams; in July, Serena becomes the No. 1 ranked player, and Venus is No. 2; Serena wins her fourth Grand Slam singles title at the U.S. Open against Venus Williams; Venus opens V Starr Interiors.

2003   Serena wins her fifth Grand Slam singles title at the Australian Open against Venus; Serena wins her sixth Grand Slam singles title at Wimbledon against Venus.

2004   Serena launches her fashion line, Aneres.

2005   Serena wins her seventh Grand Slam singles title at the Australian Open against Davenport; Venus wins her fifth Grand Slam singles title at Wimbledon against Davenport.

2007   Serena wins her eighth Grand Slam singles title at the Australian Open against Maria Sharapova; Venus launches her fashion line, EleVen; Venus wins her sixth Grand Slam singles title at Wimbledon against Marion Bartoli.

2008   Venus wins her seventh Grand Slam singles title at Wimbledon against Serena

Williams; Venus and Serena win the gold medal in doubles at the Summer Olympics; Serena wins her ninth Grand Slam singles title at the U.S. Open against Jelena Janković.

2009   Serena wins her tenth Grand Slam singles title at the Australian Open against Dinara Safina; she surpasses golfer Annika Sorenstam as the women's career leader in prize money.

NOTES

CHAPTER 1: WILLIAMS VS. WILLIAMS

1. Lynn Zinser, "A Dazzling Display by Williams Sisters," *New York Times*, September 3, 2008. http://www.nytimes.com/2008/09/04/sports/tennis/04night.html?_r=1.
2. Ibid.

CHAPTER 2: GROWING UP ON THE COURTS

1. Robin Finn, "In Tennis, Child Prodigies Whet the Agents' Appetites," *New York Times*, April 8, 1991. http://query.nytimes.com/gst/fullpage.html?res=9D0CE6DF103EF93BA35757C0A967958260.

CHAPTER 3: GOING PROFESSIONAL

1. Robin Finn, "On Tennis; Heeding the Hard Lesson of Capriati," *New York Times*, July 13, 1994. http://query.nytimes.com/gst/fullpage.html?res=9F0DE1DC133FF930A25754C0A962958260.
2. Robin Finn, "At 16, Williams Makes a Statement," *New York Times*, March 12, 1997. http://query.nytimes.com/gst/fullpage.html?res=9A00E4DB1339F931A25750C0A961958260.
3. Neil Amdur, "Venus Williams's Father Stands by His Remarks," *New York Times*, September 10, 1997. http://query.nytimes.com/gst/fullpage.html?res=9400E1DE1539F933A2575AC0A961958260.
4. *Raising Tennis Aces: The Williams Story*, DVD, directed by Terry Jervis (Jervis Entertainment Media, 2002).
5. Ibid.
6. Ibid.
7. Ibid.
8. Robin Finn, "Tennis; A Family Tradition at Age 14," *New York Times*, October 31, 1995. http://query.

nytimes.com/gst/fullpage.html?res=990CEEDD163
FF932A05753C1A963958260.

9. "Interview with Venus Williams," CNN. http://
    www.cnn.com/2008/WORLD/asiapcf/01/23/talka-
    sia.venus/index.html.

CHAPTER 4: RISING IN THE RANKS

1. Christopher Clarey, "Tennis; Williams Is Rising
    Fast, but No. 1 Hingis Turns Back Her Rival This
    Time," *New York Times*, May 11, 1998. http://query.
    nytimes.com/gst/fullpage.html?res=9803E2DD1F31
    F932A25756C0A96E958260&sec=&spon=&pagew
    anted=all.

2. Ibid.

3. Christopher Clarey, "Tennis; Seles Stays Perfect
    Down Under as Graf Wilts," *New York Times*, Janu-
    ary 27, 1999. http://query.nytimes.com/gst/fullpage.
    html?res=9F03E5DE1039F934A15752C0A96F9582
    60&sec=&spon=&pagewanted=2.

4. George Vecsey, "Sports of The Times; Cheer: 'Go
    Williams,' And Both of Them Did." *New York Times*,
    March 29, 1999. http://query.nytimes.com/gst/full-
    page.html?res=9A01EFD71030F93AA15750C0A96
    F958260.

5. Ibid.

6. Ibid.

7. Ibid.

8. Ibid.

9. Ibid.

10. Ibid.

11. Christopher Clarey, "Tennis; Williams a Pigeon
    on Clay No More." *New York Times*, May 10, 1999.
    http://query.nytimes.com/gst/fullpage.html?res=9E0
    6E2DD143FF933A25756C0A96F958260.

12. Robin Finn, "Unstoppable Team Williams Takes Doubles Title," *New York Times*, September 13, 1999. http://query.nytimes.com/gst/fullpage.html?res=9D01E6D8113DF930A2575AC0A96F958260&n=Top/Reference/Times%20Topics/People/W/Williams,%20Venus.

13. *Raising Tennis Aces: The Williams Story.*

14. Williams, Venus, and Serena Williams, with Hilary Beard. *Venus & Serena: Serving from the Hip: 10 Rules for Living, Loving, and Winning.* Boston: Houghton Mifflin, 2005, p. 6.

15. Selena Roberts, "Tennis; Advantage Williams: It's Venus vs. Serena," *New York Times*, July 5, 2000. http://query.nytimes.com/gst/fullpage.html?res=9A04E6D61039F936A35754C0A9669C8B63&sec=&spon=&pagewanted=all.

16. Ibid.

17. Selena Roberts, "Venus Williams Wins Sisters' Showdown," *New York Times*, July 7, 2000. http://query.nytimes.com/gst/fullpage.html?res=9804EEDB1638F934A35754C0A9669C8B63.

18. William C. Rhoden, "Sports of the Times; Sisters Face the Moment of Truth," *New York Times*, July 7, 2000. http://query.nytimes.com/gst/fullpage.html?res=9C05E6D91638F934A35754C0A9669C8B63.

19. Ibid.

20. Selena Roberts, "Tennis; Serena Williams Shows She Can Be Composed, Too," *New York Times*, June 9, 2002. http://query.nytimes.com/gst/fullpage.html?res=9C02EED7133DF93AA35755C0A9649C8B63.

21. Selena Roberts, "Venus Williams Wins Wimbledon, Lighting Up Centre Court," *New York Times*, July 9, 2000. http://query.nytimes.com/gst/fullpage.html?re

s=9E0CE4DB1538F93AA35754C0A9669C8B63&s
ec=&spon=&pagewanted=all.

22. Selena Roberts, "Sydney 2000: Tennis; Who Could
   Ask for Anything More?" *New York Times*, September 29, 2000. http://query.nytimes.com/gst/fullpage.
   html?res=9D00E0DE1F3AF93AA1575AC0A9669C
   8B63.

23. Ibid.

CHAPTER 5: MAKING DREAMS COME TRUE

1. Selena Roberts, "Tennis; Williamses Find Way to
   Upstage Clijsters," *New York Times*, March 16, 2001.
   http://query.nytimes.com/gst/fullpage.html?res=9F0
   0E0DA143DF935A25750C0A9679C8B63.

2. Ibid.

3. Selena Roberts, "Tennis; Serena Williams Wins As
   the Boos Pour Down," *New York Times*, March 18,
   2001. http://query.nytimes.com/gst/fullpage.html?re
   s=9505E6DB133DF93BA25750C0A9679C8B63.

4. Charlie Nobles, "Tennis; Venus Williams Escapes,
   Then Wins," *New York Times*, April 1, 2001. http://
   query.nytimes.com/gst/fullpage.html?res=9803E4D
   D103FF932A35757C0A9679C8B63&partner=rssny
   t&emc=rss.

5. Selena Roberts, "Tennis; The Night Belongs to
   Venus," *New York Times*, September 9, 2001. http://
   query.nytimes.com/gst/fullpage.html?res=9C04EED
   A1638F93AA3575AC0A9679C8B63.

6. Ibid.

7. "Plus: Tennis; Serena Williams Wins on Clay," *New
   York Times*, May 20, 2002. http://query.nytimes.
   com/gst/fullpage.html?res=9C02EFD61238F933A1
   5756C0A9649C8B63.

8. Selena Roberts, "Tennis; Serena Williams Can Now Handle the Pressure on the Red Clay," *New York Times*, May 27, 2002. http://query.nytimes.com/gst/fullpage.html?res=9E00EFDA123BF934A15756C0A9649C8B63.

9. Selena Roberts, "Tennis; A One-Two Punch in Paris," *New York Times*, June 7, 2002. http://query.nytimes.com/gst/fullpage.html?res=950DE5DC143DF934A35755C0A9649C8B63&partner=rssnyt&emc=rss.

10. Selena Roberts, "Tennis: Notebook; Serena Williams Slips, but She Doesn't Slip Up," *New York Times*, June 29, 2002. http://query.nytimes.com/gst/fullpage.html?res=990DE0D9113EF93AA15755C0A9649C8B63.

11. William C. Rhoden, "For Williams Sisters, Ambivalence Persists," *New York Times*, September 7, 2002. http://www.nytimes.com/2002/09/07/sports/tennis/07RHOD.html?ex=1230008400&en=657e46ae9765674d&ei=5070.

12. Selena Roberts, "Serena Williams Is Making Sister Rivalry One-Sided," *New York Times*, September 8, 2002. http://www.nytimes.com/2002/09/08/sports/tennis/08TENN.html?ex=1230008400&en=681c93b226483f60&ei=5070.

CHAPTER 6: KEEPING THE BALANCE

1. Interview with Venus Williams. ASAP Sports, June 24, 2004. http://www.asapsports.com/show_interview.php?id=14822.

2. Venus Williams and Serena Williams, with Hilary Beard. *Serving from the Hip*, Preface.

3. Ibid.

4. "Serena and Venus on the Fabulous Oracene, Mother of the Williams Dynasty—Mother Power— Oracene Price and Mothers of Other Celebrities— Interview." *Ebony*. May 2003. http://findarticles.com/ p/articles/mi_m1077/is_7_58/ai_100544509/pg_2.

5. Sandra Harwitt, "Big Sister Wins Battle of Williamses," *New York Times*, March 30, 2005. http://www.nytimes.com/2005/03/30/sports/tennis/30tennis.html.

6. Christopher Clarey, "In an Epic Wimbledon Final, Williams Prevails," *New York Times*, July 3, 2005. http://www.nytimes.com/2005/07/03/sports/tennis/03women.html.

CHAPTER 7: A NEW OUTLOOK

1. Alex Tresniowski, "Serena, Serene." *People*, March 19, 2007. http://www.people.com/people/archive/article/0,,20061590,00.html.

2. Ibid.

3. Ibid.

4. Ibid.

5. "UNESCO and Tour Join Forces." Sony Ericsson WTA Tour. November 12, 2006. http://www.sonyericssonwtatour.com/3/newsroom/stories/?ContentID=993.

6. Lynn Zinser, "After Trailblazer Is Honored, Williamses Carry On Her Legacy," *New York Times*, August 28, 2007. http://www.nytimes.com/2007/08/28/sports/tennis/28tennis.html?n=Top/Reference/Times%20Topics/People/G/Gibson,%20Althea.

7. Christopher Clarey, "All-Williams Wimbledon Final Is All Venus," *New York Times*, July 6, 2008. http://www.nytimes.com/2008/07/06/sports/tennis/06tennis.html.

8. Christopher Clarey, "Serena Williams Won't Vote, but Still Has Her Say," *New York Times*, November 3, 2008. http://www.nytimes.com/2008/11/04/sports/tennis/04tennis.html.

9. "Serena Williams: The Tennis Star Still Shines, Especially Off the Court," *Men's Fitness*. http://www.mensfitness.com/exclusives/239.

BIBLIOGRAPHY

Amdur, Neil. "Venus Williams's Father Stands By His Remarks." *New York Times*, September 10, 1997. Available online at http://query.nytimes.com/gst/fullpage.html?res=9400E1DE1539F933A2575AC0A961958260.

Bollettieri, Nick. *Bollettieri's Tennis Handbook*. Champaign, Ill.: Human Kinetics, 2001.

Clarey, Christopher. "All-Williams Wimbledon Final Is All Venus." *New York Times*, July 6, 2008. Available online at http://www.nytimes.com/2008/07/06/sports/tennis/06tennis.html.

———. "In an Epic Wimbledon Final, Williams Prevails." *New York Times*, July 3, 2005. Available online at http://www.nytimes.com/2005/07/03/sports/tennis/03women.html.

———. "Serena Williams Won't Vote, but Still Has Her Say." *New York Times*, November 3, 2008. Available online at http://www.nytimes.com/2008/11/04/sports/tennis/04tennis.html.

———. "Tennis; Seles Stays Perfect Down Under as Graf Wilts." *New York Times*, January 27, 1999. Available online at http://query.nytimes.com/gst/fullpage.html?res=9F03E5DE1039F934A15752C0A96F958260&sec=&spon=&pagewanted=2.

———. "Tennis; Williams a Pigeon on Clay No More." *New York Times*, May 10, 1999. Available online at http://query.nytimes.com/gst/fullpage.html?res=9E06E2DD143FF933A25756C0A96F958260.

———. "Tennis; Williams Is Rising Fast, but No. 1 Hingis Turns Back Her Rival This Time." *New York Times*, May 11, 1998. Available online at http://query.nytimes.com/gst/fullpage.html?res=9803E2DD1F31F932A25756C0A96E958260&sec=&spon=&pagewanted-all.

Contemporary Black Biography. Vol. 41. Thomson Gale. Available online at http://www.gale.cengage.com/free_resources/bhm/bio/williams_s.htm.

Dawes, Laina. "Serena Williams Talks to AfroToronto. com's Laina Dawes." AfroToronto.com. August 18, 2005. Available online at http://www.afrotoronto.com/Articles/Laina_Dawes/Serena.html.

Dominus Susan. "Dangerous When Interested." *New York Times Play Magazine*, August 19, 2007. Available online at http://www.nytimes.com/2007/08/19/sports/playmagazine/0819play-serena.html.

Finn, Robin. "Tennis; a Family Tradition at Age 14." *New York Times*, October 31, 1995. Available online at http://query.nytimes.com/gst/fullpage.html?res=990CEEDD163FF932A05753C1A963958260.

———. "At 16, Williams Makes a Statement." *New York Times*, March 12, 1997. Available online at http://query.nytimes.com/gst/fullpage.html?res=9A00E4DB1339F931A25750C0A961958260.

———. "In Tennis, Child Prodigies Whet the Agents' Appetites." *New York Times*, April 8, 1991. Available online at http://query.nytimes.com/gst/fullpage.html?res=9D0CE6DF103EF93BA35757C0A9_____.

———. "On Tennis; Heeding the Hard Lesson of Capriati." *New York Times*, July 13, 1994. Available online at http://query.nytimes.com/gst/fullpage.html?res=9F0DE1DC133FF930A25754C0A962958260.

———. "Unstoppable Team Williams Takes Doubles Title," *New York Times*, September 13, 1999. Available online at http://query.nytimes.com/gst/fullpage.html?res=9D01E6D8113DF930A2575AC0A96F958260&n=Top/Reference/Times%20Topics/People/W/Williams,%20Venus.

Gabriel, Craig. "What a Day for Serena: Champion Again, No. 1 Again." Serena Williams: The Official Site, September 8, 2008. Available online at http://serenawilliams.com/home/content/view/214/118/.

Harwitt, Sandra. "Big Sister Wins Battle of Williamses." *New York Times*, March 30, 2005. Available online at http://www.nytimes.com/2005/03/30/sports/tennis/30tennis.html.

Interview with Venus Williams. ASAP Sports, June 24, 2004. Available online at http://www.asapsports.com/show_interview.php?id=14822.

Interview with Venus Williams. CNN. Available online at http://www.cnn.com/2008/WORLD/asiapcf/01/23/talkasia.venus/index.html.

Lapchick, Richard. "Althea Gibson Must Be Smiling over Venus, Serena." ESPN.com. July 9, 2008. Available online at http://sports.espn.go.com/sports/tennis/columns/story?columnist=lapchick_richard&id=3478200.

Nobles, Charlie. "Tennis; Venus Williams Escapes, Then Wins." *New York Times*, April 1, 2001. Available online at http://query.nytimes.com/gst/fullpage.html?res=9803E4DD103FF932A35757C0A9679C8B63&partner=rssnyt&emc=rss.

"Plus: Tennis; Serena Williams Wins on Clay." *New York Times*, May 20, 2002. Available online at http://query.nytimes.com/gst/fullpage.html?res=9C02EFD61238F933A15756C0A9649C8B63.

Raising Tennis Aces: The Williams Story, DVD, directed by Terry Jervis (Jervis Entertainment Media, 2002).

Rhoden, William C. "For Williams Sisters, Ambivalence Persists." *New York Times*, September 7, 2002. Available online at http://www.nytimes.com/2002/09/07/sports/

tennis/07RHOD.html?ex=1230008400&en=657e46ae97
65674d&ei=5070.

———. "Sports of the Times; Sisters Face the Moment of
Truth." *New York Times*, July 7, 2000. Available online at
http://query.nytimes.com/gst/fullpage.html?res=9C05E6
D91638F934A35754C0A9669C8B63.

Robbins, Liz. "Noticed; Williamsmania Sweeps the Black
A-List." *New York Times*, September 9, 2001. Available
online at http://query.nytimes.com/gst/fullpage.html?res
=9A02E3D71139F93AA3575AC0A9679C8B63.

Roberts, Selena. "Serena Williams Is Making Sister
Rivalry One-Sided." *New York Times*, September 8, 2002.
Available online at http://www.nytimes.com/2002/09/08/
sports/tennis/08TENN.html?ex=1230008400&en=681c9
3b226483f60&ei=5070.

———. "Sydney 2000: Tennis; Who Could Ask for Anything More?" *New York Times*, September 29, 2000.
Available online at http://query.nytimes.com/gst/full-
page.html?res=9D00E0DE1F3AF93AA1575AC0A9669
C8B63.

———. "Tennis; Advantage Williams: It's Venus vs.
Serena." *New York Times*, July 5, 2000. Available online
at http://query.nytimes.com/gst/fullpage.html?res=9A04
E6D61039F936A35754C0A9669C8B63&sec=&spon=&
pagewanted=all.

———. "Tennis; a One-Two Punch in Paris." *New York
Times*, June 7, 2002. Available online at http://query.
nytimes.com/gst/fullpage.html?res=950DE5DC143DF9
34A35755C0A9649C8B63&partner=rssnyt&emc=rss.

———. "Tennis: Notebook; Serena Williams Slips, but
She Doesn't Slip Up." *New York Times*, June 29, 2002.
Available online at http://query.nytimes.com/gst/

fullpage.html?res=990DE0D9113EF93AA15755C0A964
9C8B63.

———. "Tennis; Serena Williams Can Now Handle the
Pressure on the Red Clay." *New York Times*, May 27,
2002. Available online at http://query.nytimes.com/gst/
fullpage.html?res=9E00EFDA123BF934A15756C0A964
9C8B63.

———. "Tennis; Serena Williams Shows She Can Be
Composed, Too." *New York Times*, June 9, 2002. Available online at http://query.nytimes.com/gst/fullpage.htm
l?res=9C02EED7133DF93AA35755C0A9649C8B63.

———. "Tennis; Serena Williams Wins As the Boos Pour
Down." *New York Times*, March 18, 2001. Available
online at http://query.nytimes.com/gst/fullpage.html?res
=9505E6DB133DF93BA25750C0A9679C8B63.

———. "Tennis; The Night Belongs to Venus." *New York
Times*, September 9, 2001. Available online at http://
query.nytimes.com/gst/fullpage.html?res=9C04EEDA16
38F93AA3575AC0A9679C8B63.

———. "Tennis; Williamses Find Way to Upstage Clijsters." *New York Times*, March 16, 2001. Available
online at http://query.nytimes.com/gst/fullpage.html?res
=9F00E0DA143DF935A25750C0A9679C8B63.

———. "Venus Williams Wins Sisters' Showdown." *New
York Times*, July 7, 2000. Available online at http://query.
nytimes.com/gst/fullpage.html?res=9804EEDB1638F93
4A35754C0A9669C8B63.

———. "Venus Williams Wins Wimbledon, Lighting Up
Centre Court," *New York Times*, July 9, 2000. Available
online at http://query.nytimes.com/gst/fullpage.html?res
=9E0CE4DB1538F93AA35754C0A9669C8B63&sec=&s
pon=&pagewanted=all.

Robson, Douglas. "Williams Sisters' Mystique Returns." *USA Today*, August 23, 2007. Available online at http://www.usatoday.com/printedition/sports/20070823/williams_focus23.art.htm.

"Serena and Venus on the Fabulous Oracene, Mother of the Williams Dynasty—Mother Power—Oracene Price and Mothers of Other Celebrities—Interview." *Ebony*. May 2003. Available online at http://findarticles.com/p/articles/mi_m1077/is_7_58/ai_100544509/pg_2.

"Serena Williams: The Tennis Star Still Shines, Especially Off the Court." *Men's Fitness*. September 2008. Available online at http://www.mensfitness.com/exclusives/239?print=1.

Smith, Stan. *Stan Smith's Winning Doubles*. Champaign, Ill.: Human Kinetics, 2002.

Supriya, Sharon. "Venus Williams: Born to Triumph." Available online at http://living.oneindia.in/celebrity/sports/2008/venus-williams-sports-biography.html.

Tresniowski, Alex. "Serena, Serene." *People*. March 19, 2007. Available online at http://www.people.com/people/archive/article/0,,20061590,00.html.

"UNESCO and Tour Join Forces." Sony Ericsson WTA Tour. November 12, 2006. Available online at http://www.sonyericssonwtatour.com/3/newsroom/stories/?ContentID=993.

Vecsey, George. "Sports of the Times; Cheer: 'Go Williams,' and Both of Them Did." *New York Times*, March 29, 1999. http://query.nytimes.com/gst/fullpage.html?res=9A01EFD71030F93AA15750C0A96F958260.

"V. Williams Interview—July 1, 2008." Available online at http://www.wimbledon.org/en_GB/news/interviews/2008-07-01/200807011214926763890.html.

"Venus Williams Bio." NBC Sports. Available online at http://www.nbcolympics.com/athletes/athlete=1049/bio/.

Wertheim, L. Jon. *Venus Envy: A Sensational Season Inside the Women's Tennis Tour.* New York: HarperCollins, 2001.

Williams, Venus and Serena Williams, with Hilary Beard. *Venus & Serena: Serving from the Hip: 10 Rules for Living, Loving, and Winning.* Boston: Houghton Mifflin, 2005.

Zinser, Lynn. "A Dazzling Display by Williams Sisters." *New York Times*, September 3, 2008. Available online at http://www.nytimes.com/2008/09/04/sports/tennis/04night.html?_r=1.

———. "After Trailblazer Is Honored, Williamses Carry On Her Legacy," *New York Times*, August 28, 2007. Available online at http://www.nytimes.com/2007/08/28/sports/tennis/28tennis.html?n=Top/Reference/Times%20Topics/People/G/Gibson,%20Althea.

FURTHER RESOURCES

BOOKS

Christopher, Matt. *On the Court with . . . Venus and Serena Williams*. New York: Little, Brown, 2002.

Edmondson, Jacqueline. *Venus and Serena Williams: A Biography*. Westport, Conn.: Greenwood Press, 2005.

Whitaker, Matthew C. *African American Icons of Sport: Triumph, Courage, and Excellence*. Westport, Conn.: Greenwood Press, 2008.

Williams, Venus and Serena Williams, with Hilary Beard. *Venus & Serena: Serving from the Hip: 10 Rules for Living, Loving, and Winning*. Boston: Houghton Mifflin, 2005.

WEB SITES

Australian Open
  http://www.australianopen.com

EleVen by Venus Williams
  http://www.venuswilliams.com

French Open
  http://www.fft.fr/rolandgarros/default_en.asp

Rick Macci Tennis Academy
  http://www.rickmacci.com

Serena Williams: The Official Site
  http://www.serenawilliams.com

Sony Ericsson WTA Tour
  http://www.sonyericssonwtatour.com

U.S. Open
  http://www.usopen.org

V Starr Interiors
  http://www.vstarrinteriors.com

Wimbledon
  http://www.wimbledon.org/en_GB/index.html

A

2000 Summer Olympics, 60
2004 Summer Olympics, 83
2008 Summer Olympics,
   94–97

Acura Classic, 29–30, 51, 79
Amelia Island tournament, 55
Ameritech Cup, 36
Aneres, 75, 103
Appelmans, Sabine, 29
Armstrong, Lance, 87
Arrington, LaVar, 80
Arthur Ashe Stadium, 7
Art Institute of Fort Lauderdale,
   54, 73, 75
Atkinson, Juliette, 53
Atkinson, Kathleen, 53
Australian Open, 46
   playing at, 34, 38, 45, 54–55,
      61, 63, 66, 69, 75–76, 81, 84,
      86, 89–90, 92–93, 103
Azarenka, Victoria, 103

B

Bammer, Sybille, 86
Bank of the West Classic,
   27–29, 68, 79
Barna, Anca, 64
Barrett, Angela Mortimer,
   35
Bartoli, Marion, 92
Bausch & Lomb
   Championships, 31, 82
Bedáňová, Dája, 69
Bell Challenge, 35
Benešová, Iveta, 82
Betty Barclay Cup, 49
Bollettieri, Nick, 22, 24
Boogert, Kristie, 60
Brémond, Séverine, 97

C

Callens, Els, 68
Canadian Open, 55, 79
Capriati, Jennifer
   matches against, 21, 26, 63–
      64, 66–67, 71, 77, 82–83
Carlsson, Asa, 29
Casals, Rosie, 22
Chase Championships, 45, 54

Clijsters, Kim, 79, 102
   matches against, 62–63, 71,
      75, 85, 87
Clinton, Bill, 52
Coetzer, Amanda, 47, 61
Common, 80
Compton, California, 26, 79
   gangs in, 14–15
   growing up in, 11, 14–15, 21,
      68, 72
Craybas, Jill, 85

D

Davenport, Lindsay
   matches against, 30, 36, 38,
      41, 44–45, 47, 50–51, 54–55,
      59–60, 62, 64, 66, 69, 83, 85
Dechaume-Balleret, Alexia, 38
Dementieva, Elena
   matches against, 60, 62, 82,
      94, 96, 101, 103
Dinkins, David, 53
Direct Line Insurance Champi-
   onships, 43

E

EleVen, 90, 103
Ericsson Open
   playing in, 55, 62–63, 89, 91,
      97, 100
European Championships, 44
Evert Cup, 47

F

Faber Grand Prix, 55
Family Circle Cup, 22, 55, 77,
   86
Fedak, Yuliana, 91
Fernández, Clarisa, 67
Fernandez, Mary Joe, 50
Fortis Championships,
French Open, 46, 55, 90
   playing at, 31–32, 34–35, 43,
      50, 56, 63, 67, 78, 82, 85–86,
      91–93
Fusai, Alexandra, 42

G

Gabriel, Rodney, 78
García, Gala León, 49
Garrigues, Anabel Medina, 96

Garrison, Zina, 57, 60
German Open, 54, 66
Gibson, Althea, 34–35, 51, 59, 92
Gimelstob, Justin, 38, 43–44
Graf, Steffi, 30, 47, 76
Grande, Rita, 68
Granville, Laura, 91

H

Halard-Decugis, Julie, 51, 59
Hantuchová, Daniela, 86, 91–92
Hard, Darlene, 34–35
Harkleroad, Ashley, 93
Haynes, Angela, 68
Henin-Hardenne, Justine, 102
    matches against, 66–68, 75,
        77–78, 87, 91–92
Hingis, Martina, 102
    matches against, 29, 34, 42–43,
        47, 50–52, 54–56, 60–61,
        63–64, 86
Huber, Anke, 32
Hurricane Katrina, 100

I

IGA Tennis Classic, 41, 46
Internazionali BNL d'Italia, 86
Italian Open
    playing at, 49–50, 64, 67, 77,
        82
Ivanović, Ana, 92–93

J

Janković, Jelena
    matches against, 86–87, 90–91,
        93, 97
Jie, Zheng, 94
Johansson, Mathilde, 93
Johnson, Keyshawn, 80
Jordan, Michael, 22
J&S Cup, 86

K

Kanepi, Kaia, 93
King, Billie Jean, 22, 60, 95,
    98–99
Kirilenko, Maria, 82, 91
Kleinová, Sandra, 83
Kostanić, Jelena, 82
Kournikova, Anna, 42, 50
Kremer, Anne, 90

Kruger, Joannette, 41
Kuehne, Hank, 80
Kuznetsova, Svetlana, 86, 92, 103

L

Laine, Emma, 86
Lee-Waters, Lindsay, 83
Li, Na, 96
Likhovtseva, Elena, 55
Lipton Championships, 42, 47,
    49
Lobo, Luis, 43
Long, Jackie, 80

M

Macci, Rick, 21–22, 24
Majoli, Iva, 30
Marrero, Marta, 82
Martínez, Conchita, 42
Mattek, Bethanie, 87
Mauresmo, Amélie
    matches against, 38, 47, 68–69,
        77, 82–83, 87–88, 93–94
McDonald's Williams Sisters
    Tour, 84, 100
Miller, Anne, 35
Mirnyi, Max, 43–44
Molik, Alicia, 84
Moody, Helen Wills, 85
Morigami, Akiko, 91
Myskina, Anastasia, 82

N

Nasdaq-100 Open, 66, 77, 81–82,
    85
National Association for the
    Advancement of Colored Peo-
    ple, 55
Nick Bollettieri Tennis Academy,
    22
Nike, 53, 79, 82
Novotna, Jana, 43

O

Olaru, Ioana Raluca, 91
Open Gaz de France, 47, 55, 64,
    77
Oremans, Miriam, 60, 63
OWL Foundation, 75

P

Panova, Tatiana, 49
Pascual, Virginia Ruano, 43, 69, 96
Peer, Shahar, 90–91
Pennetta, Flavia, 93
Penny, Brad, 73
Petrova, Nadia, 82, 90
Pierce, Mary
   matches against, 21, 36, 44,
      47, 50
Pilot Pen tournament, 50
Pironkova, Tszvetana, 86
Puma, 41, 52, 79
Pyler, James, 15–16

R

racism
   in tennis, 11, 15, 17, 34, 62
Radwańska, Agnieszka, 88, 94, 97
Radwańska, Urszula, 86, 93
Rao, Anjali, 39
Raymond, Lisa, 56, 87, 95
Reebok, 29, 44, 51
Rick Macci International Tennis
   Academy, 22
Riggs, Bobby, 99
Rogers AT&T Cup, 64
Rubin, Chanda, 31, 53, 68, 83

S

Safina, Dinara, 69, 91, 103
Sánchez-Vicario, Arantxa
   matches against, 28–29, 38,
      43–44, 49
Santangelo, Mara, 90
Sawamatsu, Naoko, 31
Schett, Barbara, 63
Schnyder, Patty, 38, 86
Schwartz, Barbara, 50
Seles, Monica, 36, 50–51, 67
Serena Williams Foundation,
   100–101
Sharapova, Maria
   matches against, 82–85, 90–91
Shriver, Pam, 101
Smashnova, Anna, 71
Sorenstam, Annika, 103
Sparkassen Cup, 70
Spîrlea, Irina
   matches against, 33–34, 38,
      44, 50

Šprem, Karolina, 86
Srebotnik, Katarina, 93
Stafford, Shaun, 28
State Farm Evert Cup, 30, 42,
   66, 77
Stosur, Samantha, 95
Suárez, Paola, 69
Sugiyama, Ai, 30, 37, 59
Sydney International tournament,
   37

T

Tanasugarn, Tamarine, 82, 94
Tauziat, Nathalie, 32, 55, 64
tennis
   agents, 20–21, 24–25
   game of, 16–17, 52–53
   grand slams, 31–36, 38, 42–46,
      49–53, 56–60, 63–64, 66–69,
      75–76, 78–79, 83–95, 97,
      99–100, 102–
      103
   tournaments, 19, 21–22, 24–31,
      36–38, 40–47, 49, 55, 61–62,
      66, 75–76, 78–79, 81–82, 93,
      100, 103
Tennis Masters Series at Indian
   Wells, 61–63
Tennis Monthly Recap, 45
Testud, Sandrine, 33, 45, 53
Thatcher, Margaret, 95
Toyota Princess Cup, 70
Truman, Christine, 35

U

UNESCO, 89
United States Tennis Association
   (USTA), 83
U.S. Open, 35, 46, 68, 79, 83, 85,
   88, 92
   1997, 32–34, 36
   1998, 43–44
   1999, 51–53
   2000, 59–60, 64
   2001, 64, 66
   2002, 69
   2008, 7–9, 97

V

Vaidišová, Nicole, 87, 90
Van Roost, Dominique, 50

Venus and Serena: For Real (television show), 77
Venus & Serena: Serving from the Hip: 10 Rules for Living, Loving, and Winning, 13, 60, 81, 84, 101
Virginia Slims tennis event, 25–26
V Starr Interiors, 73, 75

W

Wagner, Elena, 44
Watson, Lillian, 47, 66
Watson, Maud, 47, 66
Williams, Isha, 10, 80, 95
Williams, Lyndrea, 10
Williams, Oracene, 10, 13, 42, 50, 54
  charities, 75
  early life, 11
  influence of, 15–19, 25–27, 31, 57, 72, 79–81, 89, 95
Williams, Richard, 10, 33, 36, 54
  early life, 11–12
  influence of, 11, 13–14, 16–19, 21–22, 24–30, 34, 45, 47, 49, 56–57, 59, 62, 67, 72, 76, 80, 95
  love of tennis, 12
Williams, Serena, 31
  and acting, 75
  awards, 60, 71
  birth, 10
  childhood, 12–16, 18–24, 40, 72
  determination, 8, 14, 39
  education, 30, 41, 54, 75
  endorsements, 41, 52–53, 79
  going professional, 27, 34–40
  injuries, 36, 43, 50, 54–55, 59, 61, 63, 66, 77–79, 81–87
  learning tennis, 12–17, 19, 21–22, 24, 26
  matches against Venus, 7–9, 38, 42, 47, 49, 56–57, 59, 62, 64, 66–67, 69, 76, 78, 85, 94–95
  personality, 35, 38–40
  wins, 43–44, 46–47, 50–55, 59–63, 66–67, 69–71, 76–78, 82, 84–85, 90–91, 95–97, 102–103
Williams, Venus
  awards, 60, 87
  birth, 10
  childhood, 12–15, 17–24, 40, 72
  determination, 8, 14, 31, 39
  education, 25–26, 30–31, 41, 54, 72
  endorsements, 29, 44, 51, 54
  going professional, 25–38
  injuries, 43, 45, 54–56, 62–64, 67, 71, 78–79, 81, 86, 88, 91–92
  learning tennis, 12–15, 17, 19–22, 24, 26
  matches against Serena, 7–9, 38, 42, 47, 49, 56–57, 59, 62, 64, 66–67, 69, 76, 78, 85, 94–95
  personality, 38–40
  and religion, 18
  and track, 19
  wins, 41–43, 47, 49–50, 53, 55–57, 59–60, 63–64, 66, 76, 81, 85, 91–92, 95–97, 100, 102–103
Williams, Yetunde, 10, 79, 89–90
Wimbledon, 13, 46, 54, 66, 88, 90
  2000, 55–57, 59–60
  2002, 68–69
  playing at, 9, 32, 34–35, 43–44, 47, 53, 64, 78, 83–85, 87, 92–95, 99–100
Women's Tennis Association (WTA), 27, 47, 99
  ranking, 36, 43, 45, 49–50, 66–67, 70–71, 76, 83
  rules, 35
Woods, Tiger, 53
Wozniacki, Caroline, 91

Z

Zvereva, Natasha, 43
Zvonareva, Vera, 78, 97

ABOUT THE AUTHOR

ANNE M. TODD has a bachelor of arts degree in English and American Indian studies from the University of Minnesota. She has written more than 20 nonfiction children's books, including biographies on American Indians, political leaders, and entertainers. Todd is also the author of the following Chelsea House books: *Roger Maris*, from the BASEBALL SUPERSTARS series; *Mohandas Gandhi*, from the SPIRITUAL LEADERS AND THINKERS series; *Chris Rock* and *Jamie Foxx*, from the BLACK AMERICANS OF ACHIEVEMENT, LEGACY EDITION series; *Vera Wang*, from the ASIAN AMERICANS OF ACHIEVEMENT series; and *Susan B. Anthony* from the WOMEN OF ACHIEVEMENT series. Todd lives in Prior Lake, Minnesota, with her husband, Sean, and three sons, Spencer, William, and Henry.

PICTURE CREDITS